# Their
# Mysterious
# ways
## TOO

# Their Mysterious ways TOO

*More Amazing Stories
of God's Animals and Us*

EDITORS OF GUIDEPOSTS

**Guideposts**
New York, New York

Acknowledgments
"Bantam Inspirations" and "The Gift of a Happy Memory," by Renie Szilak Burghardt; "The Shedding" and "Small Miracles," by Lonnie Hull Dupont; "Love for Sale," by Nancy Gibbs; "First Love," by Janna Graber; "The Journey" and "A Home for Gus," by Crystal Ward Kent; "Gulliver Travels," by Roberta Sandler; "Love is Blind," "What Was Needed," "Unlikely Friends," "Country Surprise" and "The Delightful Mrs. S," by Lynn Seely; and "Dixie's Kitten" and "Rio's Journey," by Anne Watkins are all reprinted by permission of the authors.

"Goliath the Iguana" is reprinted from *The Compassion of Animals* by Kristin von Kreisler. Copyright © 1997 by Kristin von Kreisler Used by permission of Prima Publishing, a division of Random House, Inc.

"The Little Marine," by Joan Drage, and "Checkered Past," by Marianna K. Tull, are reprinted from *The Cat Caught My Heart*, edited by Michael Capuzzo and Teresa Banik Capuzzo. Copyright © 1998 by Bantam Books.

"Strange Bedfellows," by Marilyn A. Gelman, and "Ditto, Darling," by Ginny Greene, are from *Cup of Comfort for Dog Lovers.* Copyright © 2007, 2001 by F+W Publications, Inc. Used by permission of Adams Media, an F+W Publications, Inc. Co. All rights reserved.

Edited by Elizabeth Kramer Gold
Cover and interior design by Müllerhaus
Cover photo by Corbis and iStock
Typeset by Aptara

Printed and bound in the United States of America
10 9 8 7 6 5 4 3

# Contents

## The Promise of Love

## Ordinary Heroes

## 🐾 *Gifts of Friendship*

## 🐾 *Amazing Animals*

# Introduction

*Their Mysterious Ways Too* is about the astonishing ways in which animals interact with us humans. It seems sometimes that the dogs, cats, birds, iguanas (yes, even iguanas!) and other creatures know what we need. Of course, it is God Who is directing their actions. He knows we need love, protection and sometimes saving—and He knows as well the best of His creatures to do the job.

Each true story in this volume will inspire and comfort you—and occasionally make you laugh. Whether it's the promise of love when we most need it—or even actual life-saving—animals seem to be there for us. Whether it be dogs and cats that don't give up, even when we do—or pets who know what we need and won't take "no" for an answer—animals are our friends and ask for nothing but to have us return that love.

There is the simple majesty of God's creatures in the wild—deer, squirrels, birds, whales—that remind us that we are part of a larger plan than we might believe. We think we are in charge, but it's obvious there is so much we can't understand.

Animals are part of God's plan—they have their own lives and families, but sometimes they become part of *our* families. Sometimes God uses them to express His love for us. Do animals go to heaven? God surely must have a need for all His creatures.

# Their Mysterious ways TOO

# The Promise
# of Love

*Love animals. God has given them the rudiments of thought and joy untroubled. Do not trouble their joy, do not harass them, do not deprive them of their happiness, do not work against God's intention.*

—FYODOR DOSTOYEVSKY

# Bantam Inspirations

### Ranie Szilak Burghardt

*W*hen my grandparents—who were raising me—and I landed in a refugee camp in 1947, after World War II, our futures looked bleak. We were Hungarian refugees, who had lost our home and country due to the war. But children can find hope even in the most hopeless situations, and this was certainly true of me. Displaced Persons Camp Spittal was on the outskirts of the town of Spittal, Austria. It consisted of old army barracks as far as the eyes could see, and inside the barracks the walls of tiny cubicles, where people lived, were made of cardboard. There was a common kitchen where everyone went for their meals. There were two churches. There were barracks serving as shower and bathroom facilities. And we had our own school. I spent 1947 through 1951 at D.P. Camp Spittal, growing from a child to a young adolescent.

Camp Spittal was surrounded by another world. A beautiful, natural world of majestic mountains, clear, cold streams, rolling flower-carpeted hills, and small farms dotted with grazing animals. It was this other world that ignited my imagination with its beauty and filled my heart with hope.

My best friend, Lenka, and I slipped away from the dismal, crowded world of the camp as often as we could. We roamed the hills and valleys, explored and grew to love nature, and shared our hopes and dreams while filling our stomachs with wild blueberries or other of nature's offerings. "Someday, I am going to live in the country, in a house among large, shady trees, and I'll have lots animals around too," I dreamily would tell Lenka.

One day, our ramble took us to a farm nestled at the bottom of a pine-covered hill. The farmhouse was alpine in style, and in the neat, flower-filled yard, a woman in a dirndl frock was tossing feed to a flock of colorful bantam chickens.

"Oh, look! Aren't they adorable?" I said excitedly. Animals, whether two- or four-legged, were my passion.

"So you like my little chickens, eh?" The woman said, overhearing me. "Why don't you open the gate and come and take a closer look."

We ventured into the yard and introduced ourselves. I sat down in the grass and made little clucking noises at the small bantams. Soon, a tiny white hen and rooster jumped right into my lap and began pecking at the buttons on my shirt. The woman, who told us to call her Gerda, then treated us to generous slices of cherry strudel and tall glasses of fresh milk, and when we were ready to leave, she had a surprise for me.

"Since that little hen and rooster seem to have taken a liking to you, I decided to let you keep them," she said, setting the pair into a small crate. I was ecstatic!

"But you don't have a place to keep chickens," Lenka reminded me on the way back to the camp.

"I'll just leave them in the crate tonight. Tomorrow, I'll figure out something else," I replied, my heart filling with the joy of this new ownership. I decided to call the pair, Hansel and Gretel.

When I walked into our tiny room in the barrack, my grandfather took one look at my bantams and bellowed, "You CANNOT keep chickens in the barrack!"

"But why not? They are tiny, and I'll keep them with me wherever I go," I said, trying to be convincing. "They won't be any trouble at all."

"It's summer now, so there is no school. But what about in the fall when school begins again?" my grandmother asked.

"I don't know. But I'll figure something out by that time," I quickly answered.

"There is nothing to figure out. You cannot keep chickens here. It is too late now, but tomorrow morning you will return them to where they came from," Grandfather ordered sternly, and that was the end of that.

Later that night, as I lay in my cot in the barrack, the pungent odor of chicken litter began drifting up to my nose. So I covered my face with my blanket, still determined to find a way to keep the diminutive pair. However, at 4:30 that morning, something happened. Something that finally made me concede. For Hansel began to crow! He crowed with all the shrill might of a bantam rooster. Grandfather jumped out of bed with a thud. "What the…" I heard him grumble, while I held on to Hansel as hard as I could, for I knew his neck was in grave danger! Meanwhile, a pajama-clad crowd began gathering outside our cubicle, and they didn't sound very happy. Grandfather went out and apologized profusely, promising it would not happen again. The grumbling crowd shuffled back to bed. I dressed and quickly took the crate outside, and waited for daylight, while tears streamed down my face. Life seemed so unfair.

Hansel and Gretel were returned to the farm early that morning. When I explained to Gerda what had happened, she laughed so hard that tears rolled down her rosy cheeks. Finally she said sympathetically, "I tell you what, I will keep them here, but you can come and see them anytime you like." And that's just what I did. Hansel and Gretel seemed always happy to see me, running to me as soon as I appeared, comforting me with their little clucking noises, as if to say, "We still love you. We understand." (Ah, kids. What good imaginations they have.)

By the following spring, we received the news we had been hoping for. We were accepted to immigrate to the United States of America. I hurried to the farm to tell Gerda.

"I have heard that everyone has the chance to realize their dream in America," I told her. "That means that one day I will live in the country and then I can raise all the bantam chickens that I want."

And in America, although it took thirty years, that young refugee girl finally realized her dream, when I moved to the country in 1983. Now, I live in a rustic house shaded by massive oaks and hickories, and in my yard, the happy scratching of my sweet little bantams reminds me daily of Hansel and Gretel, who inspired a dream that finally came true.

# Unburdened

*Megan Ballinger*

Two memories stand out when Elisabeth Svendsen looks back on her early years. One is the bone disease that struck at age thirteen, leaving her right hand permanently crippled. The other is donkeys. Throughout her childhood, Elisabeth and her family drove regularly to her grandparents' house in Lancashire in the English countryside. Elisabeth's favorite part of the trip was stopping at a field where two donkeys grazed. "When the donkeys saw me get out of the car, they'd come right over and I'd pat their muzzles. They made me feel better."

Elisabeth grew up and married a businessman named Niels Svendsen. In the late 1960s, Niels developed an urge to run his own business. When he stumbled on an English country inn that was for sale, Niels realized he'd found his new career. He and Elisabeth bought the property within the week.

That summer an ad caught Elisabeth's eye. A farmer wanted a home for his four-year-old donkey. Elisabeth thought back to her childhood and the donkeys that helped her. She contacted the farmer.

When the little gray mare arrived at the Svendsens' she trotted straight into the paddock Elisabeth had prepared for her. "She explored every corner, then nudged me as if to say, 'Yes, this is nice. I'll stay.'" The new arrival, christened Naughty Face, had a habit of braying early each morning. "Maybe she'd be quiet if she had company," Elisabeth mentioned to Niels. Before long, eight donkeys were making themselves at home at the Svendsen inn. Elisabeth decided to become a breeder.

One day during a visit to a country market she found seven woebegone donkeys crammed into a pen. "One looked thinner and sicker than the rest. I assumed he was a beach donkey," says Elisabeth. "They were used as taxis for tourists to ride on in England's and Europe's coastal areas. The work was brutal, and once the animals were no longer strong enough to be useful, they were junked like old automobiles."

Just then the owner cruelly twisted the sick donkey's tail to get it moving. Elisabeth couldn't stand to watch any longer. "I went home, my mind going a mile a minute. The more I thought about it, the clearer it became. I decided that instead of breeding donkeys I would try to save these creatures of God."

By 1973, Elisabeth had thirty-eight rescued donkeys on her property. She thought her hands were as full as they needed to be. Then came the day when she received a call telling her that another donkey rescuer had died and left her a legacy: 204 donkeys!

"If I didn't take the animals, I knew they would be destroyed. I had no choice but to get a larger property where I could look after them." Niels and Elisabeth bought Slade House, a sprawling farm in Devon. One day in 1975 the headmaster of a local school for disabled children brought his students to visit Elisabeth's sanctuary. "I watched the faces of those little children light up as they reached out and petted my animals. I went back to those moments when, as a sick child, I would reach out and pat those two donkeys we passed on the way to the country. I realized the donkeys could do for these children just what they had done for me: Make them feel better."

Today, The Elisabeth Svendsen Trust for Children and Donkeys has three locations operating in England, with a fourth in the works. As many as 150 children each week enjoy a visit to one of the centers.

"The children blossom around the donkeys," says Elisabeth's granddaughter Dawn, who helps coordinate the program. "They start out petting them and brushing their manes, but with each visit comes a little bit more responsibility. Before they know it they've learned to groom and ride the donkeys." The animals clearly enjoy the program too. In fact, one donkey revels in his time with the children so much that even on his days off he tries to sneak into the center.

Elisabeth, now in her seventies, is still passionate about the program. "She feels so blessed to have found a way to bring donkeys and children together," Dawn says. "It's brought her life full circle."

# When Michael Met Rosie

*Claire Guthrie*

*W*e're getting a dog! We're getting a dog!" the kids chanted from the back of our car on the way to Pennsylvania to pick up Rosie, our new Lab, from her foster home. I glanced back at my teenager, Aaron, his younger sister, Rachael, seven, and brother Joshua, five, who hadn't stopped talking about Rosie since we'd pulled out of our driveway in Virginia an hour before. Only my two-year-old, Michael, was silent. He was just as excited, but he couldn't join in with the chatter of his siblings. I felt a familiar ache in my chest, knowing how badly Michael wanted to join in, and knowing it was impossible. It was a pain I felt often, ever since we found out about Michael's condition.

I knew something was different about Michael when he was six months old. Josh and Rachael walked and talked early. But our otherwise healthy-looking baby boy had trouble even crawling; Michael couldn't roll over and he couldn't sit up without toppling. Even more troubling, he never developed baby talk. I wondered if he'd ever speak. His brother Aaron has cerebral palsy, and I feared Michael might have a disability too. In fact, Michael was diagnosed with dyspraxia, a developmental disorder that makes it difficult to perform complex movements. Michael's trouble with speaking was part of that disorder, called childhood apraxia of speech. He wanted to speak, but his mind just wouldn't let him.

Even now, at two years and three months, he still couldn't say much more than "mama" or "dada" when he wanted us for something. And often, we couldn't understand what he wanted. His speech therapist helped us teach him some basic sign language. Even that was hard for him. A few days earlier, Michael tried to ask me for something, but he couldn't form the signs. Instead, he began gesturing wildly. "I'm sorry, Michael. I don't understand," I told him. His face turned a deep shade of red; he went into a tantrum, letting out a high-pitched scream. I felt so helpless. My baby was hurting—and I couldn't do anything for him.

I looked in the rearview mirror back at Michael, who was staring out the window. This dog, I hoped, would be something he could enjoy. My husband, Doug, and I had done our research. We looked for a Labrador, a breed known to be good with kids. A young dog, so it could grow up with our children. We found Rosie on the Web site for a Lab rescue agency. A fourteen-month-old chocolate Lab, with experience around babies, children and cats. All of our "dream dog" qualities. But would she be right for our family? Was I wrong to hope? Finally we pulled up to Rosie's foster home. I silently prayed, Please, God, let Rosie be right for our kids...especially Michael, but don't let me hope for too much.

Doug lifted Michael out of his car seat while I went to the door with the other kids. "You must be here to see Rosie," the woman said. And there Rosie was, standing in the foyer, tongue hanging out, her tail wagging wildly. Aaron, Rachael and Joshua ran up to her. "Rosie, you're so beautiful," Rachael said, ruffling her smooth fur. "Hi, Rosie," said Aaron, scratching her behind the ears. Love at first sight, I thought. But what about my two-year-old? Michael ambled over. He patted her gently on the head. Rosie nuzzled against him. I breathed a sigh of relief.

I was about to follow the woman into the other room to talk to her about the dog when I heard a voice, an unfamiliar voice. "Rosie," the voice said, strong and clear. "Rosie!" It was Michael. I looked at Doug, my mouth agape. "Rosie!" he said again, nuzzling against the dog. Now, Doug and I were the speechless ones.

Rosie sat in the back with the kids on the way home. "You're going to love our house, Rosie Pops," I said.

The kids loved the nickname. The whole ride back, that's what we called her. We were about halfway home when Michael spoke again. "Rosie Pops," he said. One word was amazing enough, but two words together? In one day? Doug and I chalked it up to Michael's excitement. Don't get your hopes up, I reminded myself. How often had I seen progress when there was none? God, I prayed once more, make this dog a good fit for our family.

A few days later I was folding laundry, watching the kids play with Rosie. Michael stood next to her, petting her as she rubbed up against him. Then, without warning, she jumped, and Michael lost his balance. I watched in horror as he fell over. I dropped everything and rushed to him. But I calmed down when I saw Michael laughing. He pushed off the carpet and stood, following Rosie again as she raced around the room. I watched more closely. Rosie wasn't being reckless. Every time she nudged Michael, she did it gently, almost as if she were testing him. And each time he fell, she waited by his side, studying him until he rose to his feet. It was a little game they were playing. A game Rosie was using to learn things about Michael.

The next night, at dinner, Michael shocked everyone when he said "juice." Right out of the blue! A day later, he said "dog." It's hard to describe the astonishment that took over our house. Over the next few weeks, he added more words: candy, cookie, car. He was also becoming less clumsy—rarely stumbling. His speech therapist was baffled. "Kids with apraxia don't progress like this," she told me.

I was baffled too. I went on an apraxia Web site and e-mailed for information. "Is there anything about dogs helping kids with apraxia?" I asked. Yes, as it turned out. Studies found the stimulation a dog brings can awaken muscles necessary for speech and other bodily movements. Each time Michael laughed, fell and got back up again, his brain was busily connecting the dots between his muscles and his actions. Now I knew why he was improving.

I went up to tuck Michael into bed. He was exhausted from playing with Rosie all day. I pulled the blanket up to his chest and gave him a kiss. Michael moved his lips. "Luv vu," he said. Did he say that? Michael spoke again. "Luv vu," he said.

I wrapped my arms around him. "I love you, Michael," I whispered through my tears. "I love you too." I shut off his light and headed to the living room. Rosie lay curled up by the TV. I stroked behind her ears and told her what a good girl she was. She was teaching Michael so much—and me as well. God answers prayers in many ways. This time He chose a dog to answer ours. Hope comes in many forms, and I must never forsake it.

# Dogs of Peace
## Lu Picard

Graduation Day! The assembly room at Children's Village, a New York residential center for at-risk teens, was crowded with spectators. All eyes were on the graduates: four large dogs—two yellow Labs, a black Lab, and a golden retriever—and four wounded veterans who'd served in Iraq and Afghanistan. My own gaze kept shifting, though, to the twelve teenage boys from the Village who, for the past year, had been training the dogs for this moment.

Actually, the preparation for this day began fourteen years ago, when my widowed sixty-seven-year-old dad suffered a stroke. No longer able to live alone, Dad moved in with my husband, Dale, and me, our two daughters, and Juliet ("Jules" for short), a wheaten terrier/Portuguese water dog mix. It was wrenching to see my vigorous father sitting on the sofa, unable to stand without help, hating to have to keep asking. "What use am I?" he'd say. "The stroke should've killed me!"

Dale, our girls and I did our best to cheer him up, but Jules was the only one who seemed to bring him any comfort. She would lay her shaggy head on Dad's lap as though she sensed his isolation.

That gave me an idea. Once he was standing, Dad could get around fairly well with his walker. Jules was a sturdy dog. Maybe if I rigged up a harness, she could pull Dad up. I fitted one end of a leather strap under her chest, the other beneath her stomach and fastened it to her leash.

Sitting down behind her, I pulled on the leash. And Jules, as dogs will when pulled, tugged the other way—lifting me effortlessly to my feet!

I repeated the routine over and over, running through a whole box of dog biscuits and adding commands. "Stay!" when I stood. "Slow!" as I took a step with the walker. After a week of practice, I went to where Dad was slumped, withdrawn and morose, on the sofa. I handed him the leash and told him to pull on it. Jules pulled the other way and suddenly, marvelously, Dad was standing.

They were inseparable, man and dog, from that moment on. Jules learned other skills—picking up a dropped pencil, bringing a magazine from a tabletop. And Dad! The simple ability to rise without calling on one of us restored his self-respect. Jules was company for Dad too in our busy household. He'd chat away to her, and she'd listen, rapt, her brown eyes alert, her tail wagging.

I believe that our best ideas come from God and that they're not meant for our own benefit alone. Seeing the difference Jules made in Dad's life, I began training dogs to help other physically challenged people. Each disability, I soon learned, called for a different kind of assistance. Balance for a child with cerebral palsy. For the wheelchair-bound, opening a door. For paraplegics, unzipping a jacket, pulling off shoes and socks. Eventually, Dale and I both quit our regular jobs to give our full attention to breeding and training dogs for this work.

And our teenage trainers? That idea too came as God's answer to a need. First, in our own family. Our younger daughter had a learning disability that made school a misery for her. I prayed for a solution. Teach her to train dogs, I seemed to hear—and we quickly discovered that she excelled at it! I watched my daughter carry herself with new confidence, and I wondered if working with dogs would help kids with more serious mental and emotional challenges. The answer was an emphatic yes.

Today, our dogs are trained at five residential centers in the New York area. Starting at the age of eight weeks, the puppies progress through "grade school," "middle school" and "high school" under the guidance of young trainers. The dogs come here to Children's Village at one year old for "college" and "grad school," learning the remainder of the eighty commands they must respond to and the special skills needed by the particular owner each one will assist.

The effect of this work on the kids is wonderful to watch. The training classroom is a concrete-block space about the size of a basketball court, with a refrigerator, washer and dryer, and other appliances that can be challenging for the disabled. I remember the first time a seventeen-year-old boy I'll call Tommy came in. Like so many boys at Children's Village who've been abandoned by their families and put into foster care or who've spent time in reform schools, he had a tough-guy swagger, a kind of armor against a hostile world.

I paired him with a golden retriever, and the first thing I told him was that it would take patience to turn this lively puppy into a trustworthy dog. Tommy, like most of the kids when they arrive here, didn't know how to handle momentary frustration. When his dog failed to respond to his first command, Tommy threw down the leash. Yet he came back the next day and the next. Three months later I watched as his dog failed fourteen times to drop a shirt from the dryer into the laundry basket. Quietly, calmly, Tommy gave the command one more time. The dog got it right. I don't know who was more overjoyed, Tommy or me. Week by week I watched him make an even greater discovery: Dogs learn not through punishment—the only kind of teaching Tommy had known— but through praise. I fought back tears the day I saw Tommy, both arms around his big retriever, whispering, "Good boy! Good boy!" into a furry ear.

He desperately wanted praise himself—they all do, these kids who've seen themselves only as failures. Each time one of them controls his temper or teaches his dog a new command, I catch them looking at me, wanting my approval.

And I give it to them, thanking them at the close of each two-hour training session for what they've accomplished. But I'm watching too, waiting for the moment when they stop looking at me, when they've developed a sense of self-worth and no longer need validation from me.

That's why, on Graduation Day, my eyes so often went to Tommy and the other young trainers. Solemnly, they led the dogs one by one to their new owners. Taking Blue's leash was twenty-two-year-old Andrew, who lost his legs in a bombing; he and Blue will go home to Minnesota. Ricky, forty-eight, has spinal injuries, but when he and Raeburn got back to upstate New York, he told me, "I won't have to bother my wife to do everything for me." Twenty-three-year-old Mary who lost both arms in an explosion, says that at home in Texas, Remi will do things she wouldn't have believed possible, "Like pushing an elevator button!" And Luis, a thirty-five-year-old Brooklyn man whose night terrors were as bad as his physical injuries, believes he'll sleep better knowing that Tuesday is curled up next to him.

I kept looking at the teenage trainers, their faces aglow with pride. Tommy, George, Danny, not one of those twelve kids so much as glanced at me! And I knew, as each one stepped forward to hand over his leash, I was seeing three changed lives—an injured soldier's, a dog's and a boy's.

# Room for All
*Ptolemy Tompkins*

*A*nimals are a lot of things to a lot of people, but to me they're one thing above all else: individuals. That's not an opinion everyone in the world shares. Researching for my article, "Do Pets Go to Heaven?" I found out just how old and how deep the argument runs between people who believe that each and every animal is a unique being with a spirit all its own, and those who believe that only human beings have souls. For such people, one dog or cat (or horse or canary or dolphin) is basically the same as another.

Very soon after that article came out, I discovered—via my mailbox at Guideposts—what side of that divide most readers come down on. I received hundreds of letters from fellow animal lovers who felt that while animals are different from human beings in important ways, each and every one of them is an irreplaceable, individual being—an unrepeatable and infinitely valuable piece of God's handiwork. Many people who wrote had lost pets and wanted to assure me that they knew—absolutely knew—their beloved animal companion was waiting for them. After all, why would a loving God exclude one of our greatest joys from heaven? My favorite letter came from a Texas rancher and "cowboy preacher" named George McVay, who felt so strongly about the spiritual stature of his fellow creatures he created a pamphlet titled, "Animals in Heaven? Yes!" that he distributed to Texas veterinary clinics and gave to friends who had recently lost a pet.

Not too long after my article appeared, my wife Rebecca's and my toy poodle, Valentine, grew ill. Early on July 4, 2005, we had to rush him to an emergency veterinary clinic. The doctors there told us what we already knew: Valentine was in a great deal of pain and that the best—and kindest—thing to do would be to have him put to sleep. Rebecca and I each placed a hand on his small, suddenly terribly fragile body, and as Valentine took his last breath, I looked into his eyes and remembered all those letters that had come in from so many people in so many different places. My article had comforted them, and now their words were doing the same for me.

If July 2005 was a difficult month in our house, August was a difficult one for the country. Watching news reports about the devastation left behind by Hurricane Katrina, I kept hearing the name "Best Friends." It was virtually impossible to watch more than an hour of Katrina coverage without seeing a van or a boat with Best Friends personnel in it, pulling hungry, frightened animals to safety.

I did some research and soon discovered that Best Friends Animal Society was America's largest—and most unusual—animal sanctuary. "They do amazing work," one animal-loving friend told me. "They even take in animals with special needs from other shelters and rescue groups."

That struck a chord. I decided I had to visit Best Friends myself. I flew out to Flagstaff, Arizona, rented a car and drove through some of the most beautiful landscape I'd ever seen to the Utah border, and the town of Kanab. Five miles north of town, I drove through the gates of a juniper-and-willow-crowded canyon that looked like it could have served as an illustration for my pets-in-heaven article.

At the main office, I met Best Friends' president, Michael Mountain—a tall, angular Englishman whose twenty-five years in the

Utah desert have done nothing to soften his crisp English accent. As a teenager, Michael was part of a loose-knit group of animal lovers centered in London. Much to his family's dismay, he dropped out of Oxford University in 1968 and started traveling the world. "Everybody was looking for the answer back then," Michael told me. "Our little group was no different. We wanted to figure out how to live a truly meaningful life. We explored many areas—everything from politics to charitable work to religion. For a few months we decided to base all our actions on the advice Jesus gives in Matthew 10: 'Go out and do good.'"

Michael and his friends weren't your average globe-wandering, fun-seeking group of hippies. For one thing, all of them had dogs. "My white German shepherd, McMuffin, and I were inseparable," Michael told me. "Traveling with our dogs gave us a spiritual anchor that a lot of other young people didn't have. We realized that our personal, individual love for our dogs had a larger meaning. It ended up teaching us what the 'good' we wanted to do in the world really was."

In the course of their travels, the group encountered stray animals they wanted to rescue. "When you see an animal that's in trouble," Michael said, "it's the only animal in the world. We couldn't stand it when we found a dog or cat that needed our help—needed a home—and we couldn't provide it."

Michael and his friends discovered what I, and all those Guideposts readers, knew so well: No animal is unimportant, or "just an animal," when you're looking into its eyes. It's God's creature. Years later when some of the old group of friends met up again in Arizona, they pooled some of their funds and purchased a small ranch in Prescott, Arizona. "We rescued dogs and cats that were going to be put down at local humane societies for lack of space," Michael said. "We'd take them back to our property and try to find them new families. Or we'd simply keep them."

So was born the basic Best Friends philosophy: Each animal is unique. Each animal is special. And no animal should ever be denied the chance to live a happy life.

Needless to say, a philosophy like that needs a lot of space to become a reality. The Arizona ranch all too quickly filled up with unwanted dogs, cats and even a few burros, bats and armadillos.

"We needed to find a larger place," Michael told me, "a much larger place." Where would we find it? How could we pay for it? It was an impossible dream. But all of us had been dreamers from the beginning, so that didn't much bother us."

In the spring of 1982 another member of the group, Francis Battista, was driving from Prescott to Salt Lake City, where he hoped to scout out some potential sanctuary properties. As night fell he found himself driving through the main street of a quaint little tourist town called Kanab. He checked into a hotel for the night.

The next morning at the hotel restaurant, Francis asked his waitress why there were so many photos of western stars hung on the walls, from Tom Mix to Clint Eastwood, just about every actor who ever rode a horse.

"They used to shoot a ton of Westerns here," the waitress told him, "at the ranch in Kanab Canyon, just outside town. But that was years ago. No one knows what to do with the place now."

Francis finished his breakfast, got back in his car and hit the road. A few minutes north of town, he passed a sign saying "Kanab Canyon Ranch." He kept driving. Forty miles up the highway, he turned around.

"The landscape I was driving through was so beautiful," Francis says. "It was literally the prettiest country I'd ever seen. And I just suddenly thought, Of course. That ranch had to be our spot." The property was even more beautiful than Francis had imagined. He drove back into town, found a pay phone and called Michael in Arizona. "I've found it," he said.

Found it they had, indeed. For the rest of my visit, under the blazing Utah sun, I traveled from one "town" in the Best Friends complex to another. In a section of the sanctuary called the Bunny House—a vast, interconnected network of hutches and open space for play and socializing—I met a lop-eared rabbit that could no longer hop because of a spinal injury. In many other shelters and sanctuaries such an animal would have been considered a lost cause. Not at Best Friends. "She's coming along a little every day," a volunteer told me, holding the rabbit in her arms. "With a little luck and a few prayers, she'll be hopping around just fine in a few months."

In a section of Dogtown devoted to aggressive dogs, I met a Katrina rescue pit bull named Daisy who'd spent most of her life chained up in a small backyard as a watchdog. "She was so aggressive she had to be tranquilized for us to transport her," a volunteer told me as she stroked Daisy's head. "But she's changing. She's always wanted to be a loving dog. But nobody ever gave her a chance."

A chance. That might be the single greatest gift that the Best Friends workers give to all their animals. When the time finally came for me to start my long drive back to Flagstaff, I couldn't help but think of Valentine, and the strange—one could almost say, orchestrated—string of events that had led me out here to the Utah desert. Is each animal unique? I believe it is. Do pets go to heaven? I believe they do. But heaven isn't just a place beyond—one that we can't reach or take part in while here on earth. After my visit to Best Friends, I understood better than ever that heaven is a place we touch right now—every time we look into a fellow creature's eyes with love and understanding.

# Wonder Dog
## Linda Rae Smith

*I*t started with small things. I'd wake up in the morning feeling weak and unrested, despite having slept through the night. Maneuvering the groceries out of my car, I'd suddenly get so dizzy I'd have to put the bag down on the ground to get my bearings again. As someone who has lived with MS for more than thirty years, I was used to coping with my symptoms. But these new episodes were distressing.

I taught elementary-age kids who had mental and physical challenges. I know what it means to struggle with tasks that others do without a thought. Helping people succeed at something they had to struggle for gave me considerable satisfaction. "But they who wait for the Lord shall renew their strength, they shall mount up with wings like eagles, they shall run and not be weary, they shall walk and not faint." Those lines from Isaiah were the cornerstone of my life.

I had always believed that my work with kids was the reason the good Lord put me on this earth. And just as I helped those kids, so God would help me. He had walked every step of the way with me through my illness, and I knew He would continue to do so.

But for once, I'd underestimated my MS. I slurred my words so badly that the kids sometimes couldn't understand what I said. My legs felt shaky and uncertain, as if they might give way at any moment.

Then a group of fifth-graders rushed past me in the hallway heading to the lunchroom one noon. I reeled and caught myself at the last second before going down. It wasn't the first time, but it was the worst. The incident shook me up so much that I was no good for the rest of the day.

I'd always taught part-time, for the pure joy of it. My husband Don's income kept our household going. Now I wondered if I could go on. One morning in class, dizzy and exhausted though the day had hardly begun, I looked at the roomful of kids in front of me. Kids with problems of their own—kids who needed more help than I could give them. I could barely get up from behind my desk. Help them? Who was I kidding? Lord, I can't do this anymore. These kids deserve more. That week I applied for disability retirement.

I did my best to stay active. I forced myself to get up in the morning whether I had anything scheduled for the day or not. I forced myself to get out of bed no matter how bad I felt. But there were days I felt so bad I could barely pray.

One afternoon, I looked out the window and saw Ritchie, the ten-year-old from a few doors down, playing with a toy truck on the sidewalk. He looked so small, crouched there under the big Colorado sky. Lonely. Kind of the way I felt. Lord, I know You still have a purpose for me. Help me find a way out of this.

"Why don't you get a dog?" Don suggested that night at dinner. "There are all kinds of service dogs these days. Not just Seeing Eye dogs. A good dog—maybe a golden retriever—could help you get around, keep you steady on your feet. You need a helper. A service dog."

A dog? Was he serious? Was that what it had come to? I got on the Internet. Don was right. Golden retrievers could be trained to do just about anything. All they wanted in return was love and support. Not much different than people, really. I found a breeder nearby. Don and I brought home a beautiful seven-week-old puppy that we named Tucson.

I had never seen such an abundance of life in such a small, furry bundle. The embodiment of joy, energy and love. Pure, devoted love. Our vet put us in touch with an excellent dog trainer. Ever hear of the movie called *The Natural*? That was Tucson. A flat-out natural. "He's a people dog," the breeder had said. She wasn't kidding. He caught on faster than I did.

Tucson's main job was to act as my "stabilizer." He wore a harness that I held onto as I walked. If I felt weak or wobbly, I'd lean into his strong body. Tucson knew exactly what to do—steady me.

Everyday activities that had become more difficult—walks around the neighborhood, trips to the grocery—were suddenly in reach again. Service dogs can't be petted while they're working because it distracts them, but everyone stopped to admire Tucson. Sometimes he'd get a little distracted by all the praise. I couldn't blame him. It felt pretty good to me too. I felt full of new energy and enthusiasm. I had my old life back!

Almost. I was still lonely without my kids. But that's all over, I chided myself.

One afternoon there was a knock at the door. Tucson trotted over to see who was there. It was Ritchie, the boy from down the street.

"Mrs. Smith, if Tucson's off duty, can he play with me?"

I looked down at Tucson. Well? he seemed to say.

"Sure, Ritchie. Why don't you two go around back?"

Tucson darted out the door and led the way. I peeked through the curtain and watched them play fetch all afternoon. Finally I had to call Tucson in for supper. "Thanks, Mrs. Smith. Thanks, Tucson," Ritchie said. "What a great dog!"

Tucson inhaled his food, drained his water bowl and stretched out on his bed with a mighty groan of contentment. I went over and stroked his head. "I'm not the only one around here who loves kids, am I?" The strangest feeling came over me. Tucson looked up at me with his kind dark eyes, almost as if saying, Don't you get it?

Those words of Isaiah's came to me again. Lord, I think I get it. I called Tucson's vet and asked if she knew of any service organizations Tucson and I could volunteer for. She suggested Denver Pet Partners, our local chapter of the Delta Society, an organization that works to enhance the lives of all kinds of people through contact with service animals.

Tucson and I went back into training—six weeks' worth. Soon after, we visited our first kids at a special-needs program in an elementary school. That first morning I walked through the front doors with Tucson. The one-of-a-kind smell that schools always seem to have unleashed a flood of emotion. I felt Tucson next to me. Don't worry, that pressure told me. I'm here for you.

We found our classroom. Most of the kids were in wheelchairs. A boy of about eight sat off from the rest of the group. Tucson padded over. The boy looked at the teacher and me, his eyes holding an equal measure of fear and excitement.

"It's okay," I said. "Take hold of his harness." The boy grabbed it, stood up and took a few halting steps forward. Tucson walked slowly and steadily, keeping pace with him. The boy stopped. Tucson looked up. It was a look of encouragement. Don't worry, I'll help you, he seemed to say. The boy took a couple more steps, each more confident than the last. "You can do it!" I cheered. I could just see the confidence flooding through him. I knew how that felt.

Today, Tucson and I visit classrooms on a regular basis. I'd say it's a toss-up who enjoys this work more: the kids, Tucson or me. In addition to his school assignments, Tucson often goes to church with me. He has proudly served as both Christmas dog—carrying a basket of toys—and Easter dog. Last year, the pastor asked the kids what happens on Easter. A little girl raised her hand and announced, "The Easter puppy comes."

Of course there are plenty of things I need help with that Tucson can't do. He can't open an extra-tight lid on a jar of mayonnaise and he can't make my voice more clear when I slur my words. In a way, though, he does make those things easier to deal with, simply by his presence—a presence that lets me know God is always close by too. Those words of Isaiah's are as true for me now as they ever were before. For only God could use a golden retriever to show how great His care can be.

# Where Bluebirds Sing Again

*Frank Newell*

*F*ebruary 15, 1986. I brought my coffee out onto the front porch of my wife Peggy's and my doublewide and took a look around. Down in the southern part of the state, where I was stationed with the military, spring was under way. But up here it was just getting started. There was a touch of warmth in the air, the grass had a tinge of green, and the buds on the trees were starting to swell. It was the kind of day in which you look around and realize it won't be long till spring and summer are back—and everything's going to be okay after all.

So why didn't I have that feeling now?

I'd been coming back to Warrenton for that "things-are-going-to-be-okay" feeling since I was a young man. I grew up on my family's four-hundred-acre farm. As a kid I spent my time cutting wood, hauling hay and milking Dad's cows. As hard as the work was, I loved every minute of it. At ten o'clock, after hours of hard work, I'd hear the same sound, the happiest one I know on this planet: bluebirds singing.

Bluebirds nested on our farm. In mid-February every year without fail, they returned from down south where they migrated for the winter. They liked the holes where the knots had turned into hollows in the wooden fence posts Dad put up. Bluebirds are territorial and need at least 100 feet between each others' nests. That's about twenty fence posts, and sure enough, every twentieth post on our property would have a bluebird nest built into it.

While I worked our fields, the mother bluebirds would work too, collecting breakfast for their chicks. Bluebirds are insect eaters. Bugs—with a modest supplement of wild berries—make up their entire diet (which makes farmers love them even more).

Sometimes, just for fun, I'd hammer together a slat house, using scraps of wood from my dad's workshop, and put it up for a bluebird to nest in. I'd even help the mothers by popping a juicy worm or a caterpillar into the mouths of the chirping babies. The mothers seemed to trust that I meant them no harm. It was small payment for all the happiness they gave me in return.

But lately, when I came back to Warrenton on leave, that happy feeling was getting harder and harder to come by. Part of the reason was easy enough to find. I would be leaving the military before too long and was suffering from a classic case of retirement jitters. What would I do when I didn't have my job to fill up my days? Was my life over? Did God still have a purpose for me?

The other reason was just as obvious. Warren County had changed a lot in the years since I'd been away. Clear-cutting had taken so many trees that there was much less habitat for wildlife. That included the bluebirds.

"It's a housing problem mostly," a local wildlife official had explained to me. "With all the clear-cutting that's been going on down here, there are hardly any trees left for bluebirds to nest in." I told the official about how the birds used to nest in the fence posts on our farm.

"Those are gone too," the official said. "Most farmers today use metal posts. They're cheaper and last a lot longer, but there are no cavities for nesting in them, so they're useless to the birds."

Those words came back to me now. It was after ten o'clock on a morning in the middle of February, but not a single bluebird was singing.

By this time the air should have been full of their distinctive, velvet-soft warbling. But there wasn't a note to be heard. Would I even enjoy life back here in Warrenton now that it was so changed from the natural paradise it used to be? No wonder I felt so empty inside. Again I wondered if God were done with me. I wish there were a couple of bluebirds around to cheer me up. My thoughts suddenly were interrupted by a familiar sound. Sitting on the branch of a dogwood just a few feet away was a gorgeous, bright cobalt male bluebird. It was chirping and twittering its head off. But it didn't sound happy. Not the way a bluebird does when it's singing for the pure joy of it. Nope, this bird was upset about something. And I couldn't shake the feeling that it was trying to tell me what that something was.

I'll bet you're looking for a place to live, I said, half to myself. Of course! That's it! I got up off the stoop and headed around back to my work shed. I hunted up some scraps of wood and hammered them together just like I had when I was a kid. Nice and simple: a square with a little hole in front that wasn't too big or too small, about the size of a tennis ball. I nailed the house to a post in the front yard and—saying a quick prayer—stood back to see what would happen.

A moment later, the bluebird was back. And this time he had company: a female, not as brightly colored as the male, but beautiful all the same. The two birds fluttered and fussed around outside the house for a minute, bobbing their heads and flashing their bright blue wings. Then, one after the other, they entered.

I went back around to my workshop and knocked another house together, then another, and put them up—keeping them far enough apart for comfort, of course. By the following week, just as I was leaving Warrenton to go back to work, most of the houses were full of bluebirds.

That was the day I officially said good-bye to my retirement jitters. I started spending every moment of my back-home vacation time building and setting up bluebird houses. Other folks got involved. One day we hammered up several different models and left them out for the blue-birds to examine. The differences were minor—a slightly smaller en-trance hole or a slightly different type of baffle tacked around it—but the bluebirds could tell the difference. They picked the same model ev-ery time. It was kind of like a bluebird focus group. (We still run these tests every now and then to see if the birds' tastes have changed.)

That was the design we used from then on. Our birdhouses started going up all over Warrenton, then requests for them started coming in from other towns in North Carolina, then from all over the country.

In 1998, two years after I officially retired, I set up a birdhouse fac-tory of sorts just outside of Warrenton.

"Frank," Peggy said one day, "I hate to say it, but you need to start charging for these birdhouses or our whole retirement's going to be gone before we know it." I realized she was right. Charging a few bucks for each birdhouse would also ensure that we could keep the supply coming. Today, we've shipped out more than seventy-five thousand houses to just about every state in the country. That purposeless retirement I'd prayed to God to save me from never showed up. A new purpose for my life did. As a matter of fact, I'm working full-time as a wildlife rehabilitator.

"Consider the birds of the air," Jesus taught us. "They don't sow or reap or store away in barns. Yet your heavenly Father feeds them."

Even the very smallest creatures in God's world count to Him. And it's our pleasure—and our obligation—to lend a hand.

# Upstaged!

*Bill Berloni*

This was it, my big break. For the past year I'd been a technical apprentice at the Goodspeed Opera House in Connecticut, spending ten-hour days lugging scenery and painting backdrops without pay. I was nineteen years old, practically penniless, and I hoped the gig would lead to my dream job as an actor. I wanted to be onstage, not behind the scenes, and I put all my faith into my dream. Now the company was casting for the summer stock production of a new musical, and the producer had called me into his office. He looked at me silently for a moment, then said the words I'd been longing to hear. "You can have a small role in the last show of the season." My jaw dropped. Finally, my prayers had been answered. "But there's a catch," the producer continued. "There's a role for a dog in the upcoming musical. We need someone to find one and train it. You do that, the part's yours. You have four weeks."

I was happy to be given a role, but what did I know about training a dog? Well, I reasoned, there were crazier ways to break into show business. "I'll do it," I said.

I drove off to the nearest animal shelter, where I figured I could find a dog, cheap. The shelter attendant led me into a room with rows of crowded cages, each with a dog, barking and crying for my attention. They stumbled on top of each other, each one begging me to take it home. I felt bad I'd have to single one out. How many times had I been up for a part, but just one actor could get the role? I found myself identifying with these poor pooches.

I almost walked right past a cage containing a small, scruffy blond mutt, dirty and cowering in a corner. I stooped down to look at him. "Oh, you don't want him," the attendant said. "He's been abused."

As I stood up, the dog crept forward, a tiny step toward me. He had long legs, crazy wiry hair and ears that flopped over on top. Far from the cutest dog in the shelter. Certainly not what you'd expect to see onstage. But behind those scared eyes, I thought I saw a spark. Something bright and engaging. More than any of the other dogs, he seemed to be pleading, Give me a chance. And a feeling deep inside me said I was the one meant to give it to him.

I reached into my pocket and pulled out a handful of crumpled bills. "It's not enough," the attendant said.

"Can I come back tomorrow?" I asked.

"Sure, but come early. He's scheduled to be euthanized." I borrowed the rest of the money and, first thing the next morning, raced back to the shelter. I made it there before the doors opened and paid the attendant the moment he got in. I walked back to the cages and found the scruffy mutt. I bent down to put the leash on. The dog backed away, shaking. "It's okay," I assured him. "Trust me." He trembled. Lord, what have I done now?

Finally, I clipped the leash on and coaxed him into my van. He huddled in a corner. "You must be hungry," I said. I stopped at a drive-through and bought him a burger. Unwrapping it, I offered it to him. But he didn't move. What if this dog couldn't be trained? I set the hamburger down. Only then did he creep forward slowly and gobble it up. We drove to the theater, and I led the dog inside. He was terrified. The crew was moving scenery into place and the actors were sitting in a circle, running their lines. But then they saw him. They fell quiet. His head hung and there wasn't a bit of wag in his tail. A stale, sodden stench caused the wardrobe person to recoil. "He smells!"

He could certainly use a bath. I filled the tub with water and coaxed him in. "It'll be okay," I said. He hit the water and yelped. "I'll be gentle." Finally I rinsed him off. The dog's dripping frame looked even scrawnier. But instead of running away, he sat by my side. "That wasn't so bad now, was it?" I threw my arms around him, not minding that he was sopping wet.

"He'll be perfect for the part," the director told me. A real-life orphan to play little orphan Annie's dog in this out-of-town tryout of a new musical called *Annie*. "You're Sandy," I named him, after his character. Every day I took him to the scenery shop while I worked. At first, he cowered at the clatter of hammers and the buzz of saws. Then one day I noticed him sleeping in the middle of the shop. I stopped and stared. At last, Sandy felt secure. Good for him, I thought. At least one of us is comfortable where he is.

I comforted myself by imagining I was an actor playing the part of dog trainer. Sandy followed me everywhere. Before long, Sandy could sit, come and bark at my commands. Onstage he was a pro. He didn't even flinch next to Annie while she sang her big number and the audience cheered. "You guys are great!" everyone said. I was happy he'd done so well. Even if he did have a bigger role than I did. After the show closed, I enrolled at New York University to pursue a major in theater. Of course, I took Sandy with me.

I'd been in New York for two months when I got a surprising phone call. "Bill?" the caller said, "It's Mike Nichols." The famous director? My heart jumped. It had to be a joke. Why was he calling me? Was he offering me a part? "I'm producing *Annie* on Broadway," he said. "Are you interested in training Sandy for the show?"

A world-famous director, and he was calling about my dog. I glanced at Sandy napping in a patch of sunlight by my desk. How could I say no?

It was a great opportunity. Sandy loved doing the show. But once again I felt let down. Sandy stared up at me with those spark-filled eyes. "You're the star here," I said to him. "I'm just a nobody." At that moment I meant it. I felt fooled by my dreams.

Ticket sales were through the roof. The show was set to be a hit. Opening night, the house was packed. I scratched Sandy behind the ears. "You know what you have to do," I said. We did a warm-up of his part. I signaled him to sit, but it was hardly necessary. He knew it so well. "Sprain a paw," I whispered. The curtain came up and Sandy trotted out on cue. He was brilliant. With every scripted bark, every time he hit his mark onstage, I beamed with pride. And the audience went wild. Applause resounded when Sandy stood in the spotlight for the curtain call. I stood in the wing, admiring him. He turned toward me, looked me right in the eyes, tongue out, tail wagging furiously. All at once a picture flashed into my mind: a scared, bedraggled stray huddled in a cage twenty-four hours from being put down. It was as if an entire plan had suddenly been illuminated for me. For the first time I felt as if I was just where I was meant to be—where I had dreamed I'd be—Broadway.

Soon more job offers poured in—training other dogs for theater, commercials, even movies. Just like with Sandy, I rescue them from animal shelters. It's the least I can do to repay Sandy for rescuing me. I got to work alongside some of the most talented performers in the business, a place I always knew I belonged. God just had His own plan to get me there. And He sent me a scruffy dog to show me the way.

# Three Little Kittens

## Phyllis Hobe

_I_n my rural area I often see barn cats hunting in the fields. In exchange for keeping the rodent population down they get food and shelter from farmers, but they aren't comfortable with people. If they wander onto my property, they run off as soon as they see me.

One morning, however, I found a cat curled up beneath the shrubs in front of my house. It was pregnant, a pretty little gray cat with black stripes. I brought out some food, which the cat gobbled up. She let me pet her and rubbed against me, purring. This was no barn cat. It was a family pet.

I called everyone in the neighborhood, but no one reported a missing cat. I tried the local police, the animal shelter, several veterinarians—with no success. It seemed probable she had been abandoned by her owners. It was also obvious that she was going to deliver her kittens very soon.

What was I to do? I couldn't bring her into my home because she might be diseased. But it was October, and though the days were warm, the nights were cold. At sunset she let me pick her up and I took her into my garage. She curled up on a pile of old towels and at that moment she went into labor.

For the next few hours I watched in awe as the cat delivered three kittens. From what I could see they were not only alive, but vigorous.

"As soon as you can, start picking them up and petting them," my veterinarian said when I called him. "That way, when you want to find homes for them they'll be ready to live with people."

Find homes for three kittens? I hadn't thought of that. I called the animal shelter, but I was told if I brought them in they would have to be put to sleep immediately. "It's the way it is," the woman told me. "The newborns and mother might have diseases our other animals could catch." There was a sadness in her voice. "If you keep them for six weeks, when they finish nursing, we can take them in then."

*Six weeks,* I thought. *But maybe I can find them homes before that.*

My house isn't large and I already had two cats and one dog, so I carried the mother and her kittens down to the basement and piled newspapers and old towels in a box for a nesting place. Of course, my other animals were curious, and it took some athletic maneuvering to get past them every time I used the basement door.

"Lord, I've got six weeks," I prayed. "I need all the help You can give me." I called everyone I knew and passed the word. I ran an ad in the local paper. I even told people I didn't know well and asked them to tell their friends. I kept getting the same response. People who loved cats already had one or more. *Surely,* I told myself, *someone will come forward.*

No one did. As the weeks passed I felt uneasy. Was God going to abandon the animals just the way some human had? I couldn't believe that. But the kittens—two females and a male—were getting bigger, learning how to jump and climb, and I couldn't keep them in the basement much longer. My veterinarian examined them and gave them rabies shots, so I knew they were healthy.

But when I called the animal shelter they had bad news for me. They were overwhelmed with kittens; they couldn't promise to keep them for long. *I can't let them be put to sleep.*

On the last day of the sixth week I reminded God that we had come to our deadline yet nothing was happening. And then it hit me: I had given God an ultimatum. I had more or less told Him I would have faith in Him for six weeks and no more.

I was so ashamed. "Forgive me, Lord," I prayed. "I know You will help me find homes for these little ones. However long it takes, I'll look after them.

A sense of peace came over me. For the first time I allowed the kittens and their mother to follow me upstairs. I trusted my very friendly dog and cats to accept them, and after a bit of curious sniffing they did.

When the kittens were eight weeks old a friend of a friend called and asked if she could see them. When she did, she fell in love with them and took one of the females home with her. Two days later I had a call from a young couple whose cat had died a month earlier. "We miss him so much," the woman said. They took the rambunctious young male with them. By the next week the third kitten went home with the young man who delivers my fuel oil.

That left the mother cat, whom I decided to keep. Like my other animals, she wasn't young and spent most of her time sleeping. But then I had a call from a friend's neighbor. "I'm getting on in years and so is my cat," the woman told me. "We need some company but neither of us can keep up with a kitten. I was wondering if you would let me have the mother."

These events happened years ago, and all four cats are doing well. As for me, I learned a valuable lesson. Now when I need God's help I simply ask, knowing He will come to my aid. And I don't give Him a deadline.

# Love for Sale

*Nancy B. Gibbs*

 $\mathcal{W}$ e've all heard it said that you can't buy love. A little over nine years ago, I proved that statement wrong. In addition, I bought love at a discounted price.

From the time I was a small child, I wanted a toy poodle. I thought it would be grand to have a dog with bows in her hair and painted toenails. I pictured myself walking my poodle down the street with her head held high. Over the years, I had big dogs, mixed breeds and scruffy dogs, but I never owned a poodle.

After I married, I continued to beg for a poodle. "We don't need any sissy dogs around here," my husband said. I realized that he was right. The last thing we needed was another mouth to feed. We already had two cats, two dogs and three kids.

One winter morning, however, I opened the newspaper. "Toy poodles for sale," the advertisement read. The words jumped out at me instantly. I picked up the telephone and, without thinking, dialed the number. It rang once, then twice, I started to hang up.

"Hello," I faintly heard.

"I'm calling about your ad in the classified section," I blurted out.

"Oh yes," the lady said. "I have two puppies left. They're adorable."

"I'll be there during my lunch break. Will you hold one for me?" I asked.

"Sure, I will," she said.

When I walked up to the door, a lady met me with a puppy in each arm. The puppy in her left arm was squirming, wiggling and barking. The smaller puppy sat very still in her right arm. The squirming puppy looked very healthy. The quiet puppy's eyes were runny and she didn't make a sound. She didn't take her eyes off me, however. I saw love in those big brown eyes.

"I'll give you this one at a discount price," the lady said, holding out the puppy in her right arm. "She doesn't seem very healthy or active, but the vet says she's fine."

"I'll take her," I said. "She's the one I want." I reached out and took the quiet little puppy in my arms. "I've always loved the runt of the litter."

"Are you sure?" the lady asked. "I thought you would want this active pup—the one with personality."

"Oh no," I said, "this one has a great personality."

That night I took my newest baby home. She cuddled up close to me. I slept sitting up, holding my toy poodle, Daisey Doodle. We were both very content just to be together.

Two days later, I became very ill, and emergency surgery was required. During the next few weeks, Daisey stayed right with me. I taught her so many tricks while I was home with her. Even though she was a tiny ball of fur, she learned to dance, to sit up and to give me five. She learned to beg and even how to pat-a-cake. My recovery time sped by while we played together.

Since then, Daisey has been my best friend. She's right beside me with every step I take. When I sit down, she's in my lap. She plays on the computer with me and barks at the screen saver. She loves me almost as much as I love her. She wears fancy bows in her hair, and her toenails are painted to match her bows.

Whoever came up with the idea that you can't buy love hasn't ever met Daisey. The lady's advertisement read, "Poodles for Sale," but I know it should have read, "Love for Sale."

My dream of having a toy poodle finally came true. Daisey was definitely worth the wait. She is also worth much more than I paid for her. I not only bought a puppy; I bought a friend, a companion and a great deal of love. I got a great bargain when I bought the sissy dog, which I really didn't need, but wanted desperately.

# Loyal Friend

*George Graham Vest*

The one absolutely unselfish friend that people can have in this self-ish world, the one that never deserts them, the one that never proves ungrateful or treacherous, is their dog. ...

When all other friends desert, he or she remains.

# Ordinary Heroes

*I, who had had my heart full for hours, took advantage of an early moment of solitude, to cry in it very bitterly. Suddenly a little hairy head thrust itself from behind my pillow into my face, rubbing its ears and nose against me in responsive agitation, and drying the tears as they came.*

—Elizabeth Barrett Browning

# Love Is Blind
## Lynn Seely

*A*ggie, my beautiful calico cat, has black and white fur with distinct swirls of bright orange segments in a few areas of her black fur. Bright white fur covers her belly and legs and wraps up under her chin to end neatly on her nose and whisker area. The end of her black tail is tipped in orange. But eyes that should have been able to observe the world are not there. She is blind. In fact, her eyes never developed due to an infection immediately after her birth, and before she came into my life. I rescued her as a five-week-old kitten; much too late to save her vision. My original intention was to foster her, then eventually find her a good "forever" home. As it turned out, I fell in love with the spunky kitten and realized she was a very special little soul. My home became her "forever" home. She has taught me many things over the years. She taught me that any impediment need not define a life, to face each day with anticipation and to live life with joy.

Aggie even showed me that love can inspire us to be brave in a most dangerous situation. One of the most dramatic ways she did this was to put her own life in jeopardy by facing a menace rather than hiding from it. She bravely attacked an intruder that broke into our home in the middle of the night. Bloody and shaken, the intruder had fled in terror!

Because of this, Aggie made the headlines in numerous newspapers and was written about in magazines and books. Now she was going to make TV history as a real life feline heroine. The fact that Aggie is completely blind made her brave deed all the more astounding. She received the "Pet Hero of the Year" award in 2002 and various other awards over the years, but this was to be her most impressive honor. "Animal Miracles" TV producers had been in touch with me and asked if they could film a segment about her.

Aggie had been invited to many places, such as the "Montel Williams" show, yet I always firmly refused as she did not take kindly to trips. But if her fans wanted to come right to her home, then that was just fine.

"You'll come here?" I asked. "From Vancouver?"

"Absolutely!"

"Well then, my answer is yes."

The morning they were to arrive was gray and brooding. I hoped it would not snow. Our driveway is long and steep and it would be difficult for them to get up it if the sky unleashed the potential it carried. That morning the weather held and I was relieved. Shortly after nine in the morning I heard a knock on my front door.

They were here.

The crew entered the house and carried in quite a lot of equipment. For a moment I wondered where it would all fit. Once they and their paraphernalia were inside, I noticed them glancing around the room, no doubt hoping for a glimpse of Aggie.

I smiled. "Please follow me and I'll show you where she is."

The star they had come to film had been dozing in her comfortable bed, a padded wicker basket, until the strange commotion of voices and thuds of equipment woke her. She did not get up but cocked her head to the side as she listened to the new noises. She knew by my voice and tone that all was well. And when all was well, then any new goings-on always appealed to her. Aggie was never one to miss an opportunity to be the center of attention, and if the visitors happened to want to admire her, well, even better. She would wait and see how things turned out.

The film crew gathered quietly around Aggie's basket, looking as if they were paying homage to a great monarch. They were concerned that their presence might upset or frighten her, but they need not have worried. "Oh, Aggie" one of the crew whispered deferentially, "you are such a brave little kitty! How courageous of you to attack a robber and save your family! And you are such a pretty kitty too." The others murmured in agreement.

Aggie's response to this heart-felt reverence was to yawn widely— though, of course, she totally agreed with them.

They all bent down, drawing closer so they could see her better. To Aggie, they were appropriately bowing in tribute while in the presence of Her-Regal-Royal-Self.

Everything was as it should be.

Aggie reached out one dainty white paw. Her diminutive wave seemed to bestow her permission for them to begin petting her royal personage. She purred loudly as they did so. I idly wondered if Aggie expected me to curtsy before Her-Regal-Royal-Self prior to her film debut. But no, she was ready for another nap. (Being regal must be somewhat tiring.)

Aggie withdrew her paw and her purr, as well as her interest in the newcomers. Then she proceeded to drift contentedly back to sleep. Her admirers would just have to wait. Right now she had dreams to dream.

An hour later the crew had the camera and lighting equipment set up. The interview regarding the night of the event began. I went first, and then my husband was interviewed. I listened as he related the incident on that fateful night.

"We were startled awake by a blood-curdling scream," he said, "and it was after we went downstairs that we saw an open window and then we saw blood on Aggie's paws. It wasn't her blood either. At that point we realized she had attacked an intruder and driven him away!" He continued, "We immediately called the police and a policeman arrived on the scene within a few minutes to investigate. He went outside and found cement blocks stacked up outside under an open window, as well as footprints in the snow leading to and away from our home. He also found a tire iron that could possibly have been used as a weapon. The oddest thing found at our house was one of the intruders' shoes. It had been left on the window sill and judging by the large indentation in the snow, he surmised the intruder must have lost it as he fell backward out of the window. The police officer said he could come to no other conclusion than the intruder had been attacked by Aggie. He was astounded by her bravery."

As the day went on, Aggie was right in the middle of it all. The crew had electrical cables and lighting stands everywhere, and most of the living-room furniture had been moved. One of the film crew asked earnestly, "How can a blind cat possibly maneuver around this stuff? Doesn't all this chaos distress her and confuse her?" Just as I was about to explain that, no, Aggie is not bothered by things being moved around, and in fact enjoys chaos, she came gleefully charging through the room, making turns and avoiding collision with the different pieces of equipment. The crew stood there, mouths opens in amazement at what they had just witnessed: a blind cat running full-speed through a new obstacle course.

Finally, our on-camera interviews were complete and the crew turned their attention to the star of the segment: Aggie. They asked if it would be possible to get Aggie to play with something or climb up and down a large cat-tree that was in the house.

"Is there some game she especially likes?"

I mentioned that Aggie had several games she enjoyed. One was to rug-wrestle. At their puzzled expression, I explained: "Aggie happily wrestles with a rug. It is in my kitchen." The producer asked if I would be able to entice Aggie to rug-wrestle so they could observe this activity before they tried to film it. "Sure I can," I answered confidently. After all, Aggie was always ready to play.

"Here, Aggie." I placed a favorite toy of hers, a large gray mouse with a bell inside it, under the small woven rug. I then moved the rug about slightly so Aggie could hear the mouse jingle.

It worked! Aggie came dashing into the kitchen, paused just inches from the rug, wiggled her backside in the air and then pounced upon the rug. She wrestled it. She clawed it. She playfully bit it. Yes, Aggie was indeed rug-wrestling! She paused every few moments and listened for the approving remarks directed her way. She wanted to make sure her audience was fully appreciating her awesome skills before she repeated her performance. "Wow, Aggie," said the producer, "you sure have the best technique I ever saw." Aggie acknowledged the compliment by showing off more of her awesome play-skills. Gripping with her front claws, she happily clawed with her back claws. Each time she did so, the toy would jiggle and the crew would chuckle.

"Okay, that's great!" the producer enthused. "Now let's get some film on that." The camera operator hoisted the heavy camera up to his shoulder. Aggie continued playing. The cameraman turned on the camera light and adjusted the focus. Aggie pounced again and played with the rug. The cameraman started to film. Aggie suddenly stopped playing. She sat up, cocked her head to one side and stayed motionless.

After a few minutes of this, the cameraman stopped filming. After all, they were on the last roll of film and he needed to be careful to get the shots they needed. "What happened to Aggie?" the puzzled producer asked me.

"Gosh, I don't know." I was as surprised as they were.

Suddenly Aggie focused on the rug and began playing again. The cameraman hoisted the camera up. Everyone was very quiet so as to not distract Aggie. But as soon as the filming started, Aggie stopped playing. I tried to encourage her by using her pet name, Aggie-Waggie. Nothing worked. However, the moment the cameraman put the camera down, Aggie seemed energized and attacked the rug.

It was strange.

Finally they asked if we could get her to climb down her massive cat-tree-jungle-gym. It was on this very cat-tree that she had attacked the robber. "Sure," I told them, confidently. "She will absolutely climb down the tree if we place her on it."

You know what happened then? Camera on: Aggie off. She seemed to know the moment the camera went on. Finally I realized that I had forgotten one important thing that would be sure to mobilize Aggie—no matter if the camera was on or not.

Aggie was sitting in the cat-tree when I took the cameraman to the side and said, "Start filming right away and you will get your shot of her climbing down the tree. I guarantee it!" I could tell he didn't believe me, but I was certain they would get this piece filmed. After all, I had a magic word to use.

He started the film rolling one last time. I then spoke the magic word softly; "Dinner."

Suddenly Aggie bolted into animation! I smiled as I watched her navigate the complex levels of the seven-foot-high jungle-gym-cat-tree at the speed of light! Down she came, the camera finally capturing her action.

Success! Everyone cheered! They got their footage and Aggie got her reward—food!

When the film crew was ready to leave, they came over, one by one, and bowed down to give Aggie a good-bye pat on the head. "By the way," the producer said just before she closed the front door, "someone should make a full-length movie about her. The thing is, it would be impossible to find another cat like Aggie to play the part."

Aggie waved her fluffy tail in complete agreement, before curling up on the sofa for a nap.

It had been an interesting day for her, to be sure. A few minutes later I noticed her whiskers twitching. She was dreaming. Images of rug-wrestling were dancing across her mind.

Or perhaps, as she laid dreaming, she was once again defending her home from a very dangerous menace—and once again saving the family she so dearly loved.

# Family Hero

*Pam Sica*

*H*ow old is Bullet now?" the vet asked as he lifted our old golden retriever up on the examination table. "Thirteen," I said. He put his stethoscope on Bullet's shaggy chest and leaned forward. "I don't like what I'm hearing," he said. "I'll have to do an electrocardiogram."

The EKG led to a blood test, which led to the discovery of a growth on his liver. The vet's prognosis was grim: If we didn't operate soon, Bullet would die. The cost of the operation, including sonograms, X-rays, bloodwork and medicine would be costly. "I know how much Bullet means to you," the vet said, "but the average lifespan of a golden retriever is ten to thirteen years. Why don't you go home and think about what you want to do?"

On the way home I stopped by the grocery store where I bumped into a neighbor and explained my dilemma. "Pam," she said, "the dog is thirteen years old. He's had a good life. Let him go."

"I can't. Bullet is family. We've been through everything together."

He had arrived at my doorstep in a wicker basket wearing a red bow—a gift from my husband to save our faltering marriage. Bullet had shiny brown eyes and thumped his tail. The marriage did not work, but Bullet stayed. On nights when I returned home late from my restaurant job, Bullet would nuzzle me and rest his chin reassuringly on my lap.

By the time I was ready to start dating again, he became my best chaperon. If he didn't like a guy, his tail drooped and he refused to be petted. For those lucky ones who passed muster, he'd wag his tail, fetch his favorite chewed-up groundhog toy, deposit it at the guy's feet, then look over at me as if to say, "This one might be okay."

Several years later, a new part-time security guard named Troy started working at the hotel restaurant where I worked. One snowy night near closing time, one of the gals and I were having some hot chocolate. Troy waltzed in, covered with snow. "Looks good," he said. "Could you make me some?"

Something about his attitude made me snap back, "Kitchen's over there. Make it yourself."

My friend chided me for being rude, but I was unrepentant. Out in the parking lot the snow was piled in three-foot drifts. I scraped it off my Oldsmobile Cutlass, got in and turned the key. Nothing doing. I tried again and again, my fingers near freezing. Feeling pretty sheepish, I headed back to the hotel to find our new security guard.

"I think my battery is dead," I told him. "Do you have some jumper cables?"

Troy's brown eyes danced, and he could barely suppress a grin. "Do you mean you want me to help you?"

My Cutlass refused to start, and Troy had to give me a lift home. No sooner had he dropped me off than he was ringing my doorbell. His truck was stuck at the end of my driveway, and he had to sleep on my couch with Bullet standing guard.

The next morning he shoveled my front walk and driveway, got his truck running and drove to the convenience store around the corner. He returned with steaming coffee, orange juice and doughnuts. We sat around the kitchen table. Bullet wagged his tail and licked Troy's hand. He brought his old stuffed groundhog toy and dropped it in Troy's lap. Bullet didn't want this one to get away. Neither did I.

All the happiness that I had missed in my first marriage I found with Troy. He was funny, kind and as much a dog-lover as I was. We looked forward to raising a family. Unfortunately, whenever I conceived I couldn't carry a baby past two months.

"That's all right," we told each other. "We have Bullet." We took him to the park, to Florida, to the beach—all those things you do with a kid. We bought Christmas presents for him and celebrated his birthdays.

That's why it was devastating to contemplate his loss. "The vet says that the tests and the operation will cost a fortune," I told Troy after Bullet's exam. "But I don't see any other choice. Bullet helped me when I was at my lowest. Now I need to help him."

Before the surgery we took Bullet to our parish priests. Father Mike and Pastor Ryan said a prayer and blessed him. I prayed, Dear God, if you still have some purpose for him, don't take Bullet from us. Not yet. Please.

The surgery was a success. Bullet came home and in a matter of weeks he was his old self again. Of course, he moved a little slower and wasn't as fast at fetching his chew toy, but then I didn't run after him as quickly as I used to. He might have been thirteen, but I was forty.

That summer I experienced some recurring nausea I wrote off to indigestion. Troy talked me into taking an over-the-counter pregnancy test. The test was positive! We hugged and laughed and cried while Bullet ran around us carrying the empty pregnancy test box in his mouth like a trophy.

Troy Joseph was born on April 10, 2002. We'd done all we could to prepare Bullet for the addition to the family, showing him the crib and the changing table and the baby clothes we'd been given. The nurse on the maternity ward suggested getting him accustomed to the smell of the baby. "Take your dog one of little Troy's blankets so he can get used to his scent."

Later that night Troy called me at the hospital from home. "You're not going to believe this. I gave Bullet the blanket and he won't let go of it. Right now he's all curled up sleeping with it."

We brought Troy home and set him in his car seat on the living room floor. Bullet came over to investigate. He looked, sniffed, wagged his tail. No matter where I took the baby, Bullet was by our side. Even at night, instead of sleeping at the foot of our bed, Bullet curled up next to the crib. Little Troy was his.

On the morning of May 1, we were awakened at four o'clock by Troy's alarm. He was going back to work for the first time since the baby was born.

"You get ready," I told him. "I'll take care of the baby."

I changed Troy Joseph's diaper and put him on our bed. Bullet stayed in our bedroom while I went to the kitchen to warm a bottle. I was standing at the kitchen sink, testing the milk on my wrist, when Bullet came barreling down the hall, jumping and barking furiously.

"Want to go out?" I asked. I opened the door, but he wouldn't budge. He stared at me with pleading eyes, barked, then tore back down the hallway. Crazy dog! I followed, stopping at the bathroom to ask Troy to test the temperature of the milk. Bullet returned, barking with a vengeance.

"What's the matter with him?" Troy asked.

"I don't know. He doesn't want to go out."

In our bedroom Bullet sat whimpering by our bed. By the glow of the nightlight I could see the baby's head thrown back in an odd way. He was making faint gurgling noises. I picked him up and watched in horror as he went from purple to blue, then limp in my arms.

"Troy!" I screamed and dashed to dial 911. "The baby's stopped breathing!" Troy tried to do CPR until the police and EMTs arrived. Bullet followed them in, barking frantically. I had to drag him into the kitchen and barricade the door with two chairs so he couldn't get out.

The EMTs managed to resuscitate our baby before they whisked him off in the ambulance. His father rode with him, and I followed in the truck. For the next sixteen days Troy stayed in the pediatric intensive care unit. After countless tests later it was determined that Troy's breathing problem was caused by double pneumonia and undiagnosed heart irregularities.

"You're lucky you found your baby when you did," said the doctor. "Had any more time passed, he most likely would not have survived."

Troy Joseph is doing fine now. We monitor his situation with frequent doctor visits. As for Bullet, I thank God for every day that he's still around. He's more than a hero in our house. He's an answer to prayer.

# Jeremy's Choice

## Marion Bond West

$\mathcal{I}$ closed my journal, put down my pen and dialed my son's number. Quite possibly he'd refuse to answer. Or, if he did, I'd probably have to do all the talking. One ring, two, three...Pick up, Jeremy. Just so I'll know you're alive.

"'Lo."

"Hey there. What are you doing?" I chirped.

"Nothing."

"How are you?" Silence. The long familiar silence. "Would you like to...?"

"I gotta go, Mom." Click.

I put down the phone and stared at a childhood picture of Jeremy, remembering his red hair, freckles, his eyes, his laughter. The clown in the family. His father's death when he was fifteen had hit him hard, but he kept his grief to himself, locked up someplace no one could get to, not even him. I never saw tears. He took over caring for our large yard, the yard his father tended so well, and kept it perfect. Yet that perfection also felt like denial. Eventually he started his own landscaping business. He prospered. I thought he was doing well.

In his thirties things changed. At the time I didn't understand it. He would sleep at odd hours or not at all. He started spending money recklessly, buying crazy things he had no use for, like window blinds that didn't even fit his house. Then he stopped taking calls from family and he surrounded himself with unsavory characters. By the time we realized that he was into drugs there seemed to be nothing my husband Gene or I could do. The only thing that Jeremy seemed connected to was a white Persian named Snowy. He took after me in that respect—we were both devoted to our animals.

One day we rushed to the ER because Jeremy had been in a car wreck—again. We found him lying in bed behind a white curtain, looking hopeless. "Mom," he said, "hurry to my house and see if Snowy is still okay. Put him in his carrier and get him out of there before someone steals him. People have been taking my things."

Of course, I thought, you leave the doors unlocked and all kinds of strangers help themselves to whatever. But now was no time to lecture. I drove over to Jeremy's litter-strewn house. There was no big white cat or even a cat carrier. Snowy was gone.

I went back to the hospital to tell Jeremy. But I didn't have to. He took one look at my face, then turned to the wall and cried uncontrollably, as if a dam holding back years of loss and grief and pain had finally burst. Shortly thereafter he reluctantly agreed to enter a psychiatric rehab facility. I visited often, yet Jeremy refused to make eye contact. All he said was, "Get me out of here."

The psychiatrist diagnosed him as bipolar. "With the right medicine we can help him a lot," the doctor said. "And what he needs to do is to stay in counseling."

I held my breath after Jeremy's release. In a few months I was scrawling in my journal: Jeremy hasn't been taking his meds regularly. And he keeps breaking appointments with his counselor. I have no idea what to do, Lord, except place him in Your hands—again. Could You show me some way to help him? I picked up the phone that morning and called him. The short conversation in which he spoke in monosyllables followed. Then click.

That click was almost like a slap. Stinging, accusatory.

Later that day I stopped at a pet store to buy food. I felt eyes staring at me. I turned and spotted a magnificent full-grown white Persian cat. I pulled out my cell phone and dialed Jeremy immediately. I had to speak fast, before he had a chance to hang up.

"Jeremy," I blurted out, "I'm looking at the most wonderful white Persian cat. Let me get him for you. Please."

"No way. Forget it. I don't want to have to take care of anything. I don't want to love anything ever again." Click.

In my journal I wrote: Lord, please show me a way to give Jeremy a cat. Help us. Soften his heart.

I couldn't give up. I knew that sometimes when you can't love yourself or even anyone else, all you can love is an animal, something that will accept your love unconditionally. I checked the want ads faithfully. One day I read, "Persian kittens for sale." I dialed the number. The woman lived near Jeremy. She agreed to meet Jeremy and me at a fast-food place close to Jeremy's new apartment. Then I phoned my son. "I have something to show you," I said. "Can we meet?" Long pause. I braced for the click.

"Okay, Mom."

A chilly wind blew and the overcast sky remained a hopeless gray. I sat in my car, waiting for a stranger in a yellow SUV and Jeremy in his truck. The two pulled up at the same time. I took that as a good sign. Jeremy climbed out of his truck slowly. He walked over to my car, head down, still limping from the accident.

I hopped out and threw my arms around him. It was like hugging a telephone pole. He didn't even take his hands out of his pockets. "What do you want?" he asked, avoiding my eyes. Just then the lady walked up with four kittens snuggled in a blanket—black, beige, orange and most important, white.

She spoke immediately. "Hi, Jeremy. Your mom says you love cats. Well, these cats really need good homes." She could have been holding live snakes the way Jeremy jerked back suddenly. He just stared. Then, slowly, he reached out and touched the white one on its mushed-in little pink nose.

"Hold him," the woman insisted. I took the other three while she put the white kitten into Jeremy's large hand. She closed his fingers around it one by one. The little thing shivered in the wind. Jeremy tucked it inside his jacket close to his heart. At that moment the wind died down and I could hear a gentle purr.

For an instant Jeremy's eyes met mine—the first time in years, it seemed.

"That one's meant for you," the lady said.

Jeremy turned. We watched him walk slowly to his truck, the kitten inside his jacket. I paid her and hugged her hard, then ran to catch up with Jeremy. I tossed a bag of cat food and a cat bed into his truck and waved good-bye. Don't hover, I told myself. Don't even call. Be patient and wait for Jeremy to call you.

A week later Jeremy finally did. His voice was animated. "Mom! You'll never guess what. I lost that little kitten when I first brought him home. I finally found him in a drawer—like a little Houdini. That's what his name is. Do you like it?"

"Yes." It was suddenly the most beautiful name in the whole world.

"I got a job—nothing big—but I need to work so I can take Houdini to the vet and the groomer. He rides around in my truck with me. And he sleeps with me." Tears plopped down on my shirt like fat raindrops. "Mom, I've started back seeing my doctor and counselor. I'm going to join a therapy group. I need to talk to other people. I'll die if I don't."

I nodded, wiping my nose.

"I can make it. I know I can. Anyway I called to thank you. I started painting my apartment. Maybe you can stop by sometime. You wouldn't recognize Houdini. He's so big...."

I didn't say so, but he was wrong. I would recognize Houdini. Love is always unmistakable.

# Trouble in the Night

*Kristin von Kreisler*

$G$oliath, a four-foot-long emerald-green iguana with skin the texture of a football, nestled under Duane Wright's chin in Tucson, Arizona. He murmured to the reptile, whom he's named Goliath before he realized that she was a female, "You're my good girl. I love you!"

Goliath snuggled closer against his neck as if to say, "I love you back." Or at least that's what Wright felt she was conveying.

This exchange was not their only way of showing affection. When Goliath first came to live with Wright, she sneezed.

"I love you too!" he patted her.

Soon she crawled on his shoulder many times a day and sneezed in his face, he believed, to express her tender feelings for him. For hours she lay across his chest, stretched out her arms, and rested her cheek against his shirt as if she were trying to hug him.

"Iguanas are extremely loving if you love them," Wright told his wife, Arlene.

Goliath, who had fiery brown eyes and sharp little claws, was Wright's companion twenty-four hours a day, seven days a week. She was the only fur-and-dander-free pet the doctors allowed him. Because of his asthma, chronic lung diseases and sleep apnea, Wright was confined most of the time to one room of his house, near machines administering lung medication every few hours and controlling humidity and temperature. During the day, he lay on his bed or recliner with Goliath tucked close. At night he and Goliath slept near an intercom, so that Arlene could monitor his breathing from another room.

One evening Wright wasn't feeling well. Instead of taking Goliath to bed as usual, he tried to dislodge her from his chest and put her on the special stand he'd created from a computer desk. The stand had all of the comforts that he imagined an iguana would appreciate: branches for her to climb in, little pillows and a heating pad to lie on, and even a water bowl, made from a kidney-shaped hospital spittoon, which Wright had covered with plaster of paris and painted black to resemble a rock, so that she'd feel at home.

That night Goliath would have nothing to do with her special perching place. She wouldn't loosen her claws from Wright's shirt and let him go to bed alone. Instead, she insisted on accompanying him and cuddled up across his chest in her usual spot. He patted her, settled under his blanket, and fell asleep.

About 1:30 in the morning, he vaguely sensed that Goliath was whipping his face with her tail. But Wright was too sleepy to respond. When he didn't open his eyes, she clawed and bit his face. She was clearly determined to rouse him. As he slept on, she whipped and clawed and made such a fuss that Arlene finally heard her on the intercom.

Arlene hurried to Wright's room to find out what the disturbance was. Just as she entered, Goliath finally succeeded in awakening him. Choking for air, he had stopped breathing. (The iguana maybe sensed this coming before Wright had even gone to bed.)

As Goliath watched, her mission accomplished, Arlene helped Wright to a respirator. When his breathing improved, she took him, sick and woozy, to the hospital, where doctors administered oxygen and intravenous prednisone, which cleared his lungs.

Wright told the doctors that Goliath had rescued him; she'd been concerned about him. "You can't help but love an animal that saves your life," he said.

Eager to see his protective iguana, Wright returned home to find Goliath resting on her branch on the computer desk, her green tail hanging in the spittoon water bowl. She was waiting for him.

# Lucky Enough!

### Victoria Ries

$\mathcal{I}$ was uncomfortable the minute the man pulled up to the house in his beat-up pickup truck. He looked like a cowboy who had been out on the range too long, wearing a soiled vest and a Stetson hat, unshaven, his bloodshot eyes darting nervously while talking to me. I might have told him to leave right then had it not been for that cute dog that was with him.

He was a handyman who'd come by a couple of days earlier looking for work. Me, trust a strange man at my house? Not usually. Especially now. But I was desperate. Don't get me wrong, the kids and I loved living the quiet life in the beautiful, unspoiled White Mountains of eastern Arizona, far from the hustle and bustle of Phoenix. But three years after we moved out here, my husband and I divorced. He moved on. Now I was all alone, raising two kids (three-year-old Victoria and one-year-old Travis) on a shoestring budget, twenty miles from the nearest town, half a mile from my closest neighbor. God forbid a fire broke out or some other kind of emergency came up. It scared me. I worried all the time. Anyway, I needed a fence put up and some carpeting laid. The man's price was right. Then again, you get what you pay for, I suppose, and now I was second-guessing myself.

"What's her name?" I asked, reaching down to pet the pup.

"Lucky," the man grunted, then spit. "My kids found her under a pine tree when they were hiking in the woods. Now I'm stuck with her."

Lucky cringed when I touched her. "Don't worry, I'm not going to hurt you," I said softly. I ran my hand through her velvety fur. Her whole body tensed. Lucky looked up at me with her big eyes, like there was something she was trying to tell me.

The man finished with the fence and was ready to lay down the carpet. But first he unwrapped a sandwich and bit into it. Lucky stared, her tongue hanging out. "Can I get your dog something to eat?" I asked.

"I wouldn't," he growled between bites. "You'll never get rid of her."

Real nice, I thought, and as soon as he started on the carpet, I snuck outside with Lucky and got her something to eat and drink.

When he was done, the man went over to his pickup truck and opened the door. "C'mon now, dog," he yelled. Lucky wouldn't budge. She cowered behind my legs. I could feel her heart beating. I could feel mine too. The man came toward me. He grabbed Lucky by the collar. Then he kicked her toward the open door, muttering under his breath the whole time. He picked her up and threw her onto the seat. Lucky landed with a yelp. The man didn't even bat an eyelid as he climbed inside.

I ran over to the truck. "Wait!" I yelled. The man rolled down his window. "If you don't want that dog, I'll take her!" I said, half pleading, half demanding.

"The kids would throw a fit," he muttered, and without looking me in the eye, drove away down the dirt road. I could see Lucky in the cab's rear window, staring forlornly at me.

I told myself the situation, hard as it was, was none of my business. But I couldn't get that sad image out of my mind. While lying in bed that night I could see her pleading brown eyes. Finally I decided I would have to turn the whole thing over to God, asking Him to protect that poor puppy. "Please help Lucky." Then I added, "And please keep an eye on my children and me too. Amen."

It wasn't more than a minute or two later that I heard a strange scratching sound coming from the front door. I sat up in bed, startled. I went to the door and opened it. Lucky! She wagged her stumpy tail and stared up at me. I knelt down and she licked my face, then tore inside. I followed her in, gave her food and water and rubbed her tummy. Finally she stretched out at the foot of my bed and fell asleep. That's when reality set in. I had enough on my plate with two kids, three dusty acres and no husband to help. And what about that handyman? He was sure to come looking for her. He would probably accuse me of stealing her.

The next morning Lucky romped through the yard with Victoria and Travis. When they toddled toward the woods, Lucky shepherded them back to the house, like they were her own little charges. I don't know how you got here, I thought, but I can't let you go.

Still, I dreaded the man coming back. And he did. Three days later there was a knock at the door. "I came for the dog," he said. I was about to tell him off, but Lucky did the talking for me. She growled and bared her teeth. The man lunged for her. She snapped at him. He backed away. "Heck, you can have the no-good ungrateful mutt," he said, then jumped into his truck and drove off. Lucky gazed up at me, tail wagging, her pink tongue hanging out.

"You're part of the family now," I assured her. Still, I had that little bit of apprehension in the back of my mind about being out here all alone, even with Lucky. After all, she was just a cute little dog. Lucky is safe, but what about us?

One snowy night about a year later, I was sleeping soundly in my bed. A nudge to my shoulder woke me up. "Lucky, stop," I said. "No play." I drifted off. She pawed my shoulder once more. I rolled away from her. She let out a short, sharp bark. I ignored her, trying to sleep. Then she licked my face.

"Okay! I'm up, I'm up!" I said. Then I opened my eyes. The air was hazy. I immediately started coughing. Smoke!

Barefoot, I ran to wake the kids and carried them, one in each arm, outside to the car, Lucky at my heels. We stood at a safe distance, looking at the house. I couldn't see any flames. I put a bandanna over my nose and mouth and went back inside. That's when I discovered the source: a pine log smoldered in our woodstove. Apparently, the chimney was clogged. With all the windows shut on a cold night, the smoke had backed up into the house. If it hadn't been for Lucky...

The four of us snuggled in the car, waiting for the smoke to clear out from the house, the kids and I taking turns hugging and praising Lucky.

It's funny how prayer works, and how we are protected in ways we could never even imagine.

# Some Service Dog

*Brenda Mosley*

$\mathcal{S}$omething poked me in the face. Something cold and wet. "Not again, Toby," I moaned groggily, pushing my dog's nose away from mine. I rolled over. Just as I was falling asleep again, he nipped at my sleeve. "Toby, stop!" I commanded. He flopped down next to my bed and promptly started snoring. I didn't even care about the noise. Maybe I'd finally be able to get some sleep myself. I drifted off.

A tug on my foot. What now? I forced my eyes open. Toby was trying to pull off my sock. I nudged him away, glaring at him. He cocked his head and looked at me quizzically. My alarm clock hadn't gone off yet. It was only five. I'd been planning to get up early for my doctor's appointment, but not this early. Would this dog ever learn?

Every night for weeks now he'd been waking me up. Not just once or twice. Constantly. I couldn't remember the last time I got a good night's rest. And, Lord knows, I needed it. Living with both cerebral palsy and multiple sclerosis was debilitating. If my old service dog were still around, I might have coped, but Toby? All I'd been able to train him to do so far was fetch my slippers. Some service dog! I needed help with a lot more than that.

My old dog, a retriever named Farley, had only taken basic obedience lessons when he came to live with me. I'd never trained a dog before, but he was so smart it didn't take long for me to teach him to do all kinds of things around the house. Farley would bring me the phone, get a can of soda from the fridge, take clothes out of the dryer. He carried grocery sacks, helped me up from chairs, steadied me if my walk got wobbly. He even pulled me in a wheelchair those times I had to use one.

For ten years he was my companion, my partner. Together we helped other people with disabilities train their service dogs. Thanks to Farley, I'd been able to avoid the fate I dreaded—moving into an assisted-living center—even after my condition deteriorated so much that I had to quit my job teaching preschool and go on disability. He was a real answer to prayer, my Farley. A champion service dog.

I was inconsolable when he died. What dog could ever replace him? But I knew that if I wanted to continue living on my own, I'd have to get a new service dog. So I went to a kennel, hoping I would find another answer to prayer. Yet even I couldn't quite believe the retriever I spotted in an outdoor run. He looks just like Farley! Long legs, reddish fur and all. Toby was his name, the kennel owner said.

I took Toby for a test walk on a gravel path, a tricky surface for me. He walked beside me slowly and deliberately, seeming to sense my hesitation. Good temperament, I thought. The only drawback: Ideally, a service dog is fully trained by age two, and Toby was already four.

But Toby's uncanny resemblance to Farley...what else could he be but another answer to prayer? I bet I can teach him to act like Farley too, I thought. I had a good track record when it came to training service dogs.

I brought Toby home. The first thing he did was tear through every room in the house. "Stop!" I ordered. He paused, looked at me, then bolted through the doggy door to the backyard.

Toby had been kenneled outdoors his whole life. It would take time for him to adjust to living in my house. I just didn't expect it to take this long. Everything scared him. When the phone rang, he howled and cowered in a corner. When the dryer buzzed, he ran for cover. When the deliveryman knocked on the door, Toby jumped a mile high, barking frantically.

Toby's sole talent seemed to be napping. He would drop off right in the middle of a training session. Once I spent an entire morning rolling a tennis ball across the floor. "Fetch," I said. Sometimes Toby grabbed the tennis ball in his mouth, but he wouldn't bring it back to me. Aren't retrievers bred to do this? I decided to try something softer. Maybe it would be easier for him.

I dropped one of my fuzzy slippers near him. "Get the slipper, Toby." Toby ignored the slipper, walked over to me, put his head on my leg and yawned. "Off," I said, pushing his head gently toward the floor. "Get the slipper." Toby curled up at my feet and dozed off.

Something in me just snapped. "Toby," I called. Loudly. He jolted awake and looked at me. I bent down. "This is a slipper!" I yelled. I pushed it into his mouth. "How could I have ever thought you were an answer to prayer!" I got up, stumbled into the bathroom and slammed the door.

I stared at my reflection in the mirror. I looked drained. The MS was making me weaker and weaker. Dogs don't respond well to anger, I reminded myself. You've got to try again with Toby. You don't have the strength to start over with another dog.

I opened the door. Toby sat in the exact spot I'd left him. His tail wagged. He still had the slipper in his mouth. I didn't know whether to laugh or cry. "Drop," I said. Right away he did. "Good dog!" I patted his head. He spent the rest of the day happily retrieving my slipper.

But that was all he learned in two months of training. I couldn't count on Toby day-to-day. Certainly not in an emergency. I couldn't count on him for anything, really, except waking me up at night, practically every night.

And I've had enough of that, I thought, swinging my legs over the edge of my bed and sitting up. I eyed my so-called service dog. Toby sprawled on the floor, apparently satisfied that he'd successfully kept me from yet another night's rest. Lord, You couldn't have meant this dog for me.

I stuck my feet into my slippers and stood. Might as well get ready for my doctor's appointment. Prepare myself to tell her I'd made the decision I had dreaded my whole adult life. I was going to give up my dog, my house, my independence. Could she help me find a place in an assisted-living center?

Later that morning my doctor ushered me into her examination room. "Are you okay, Brenda?" She said with concern. "You look tired."

"That's because I'm not sleeping."

"Why not?" she asked.

I told her about my problems with Toby. "Maybe he's just acting out because I've been working him so hard," I said. "But I wouldn't have to if he'd just learn."

My doctor listened to my lungs, then checked my nose and throat. "It might be good that Toby's been waking you."

"Good?"

"You're showing signs of sleep apnea. People with this condition stop breathing during the night. Left untreated, it could lead to a heart attack or stroke." She set up an appointment for me at a sleep clinic the following week.

Toby and I went to the clinic together. They said it was okay since he was a service dog. My bedroom for the night was connected to a control room, where observers would monitor me while I slept. Normally that would've bothered me. But I was too tired to care. A nurse attached electrodes to my head, chest and legs. I stretched out on the bed and Toby curled up on the floor beside me. As usual, he conked out right away. Well before I did.

And as usual, Toby barely let me sleep a wink. He'd get up to lick my hands and snort in my face. He's hopeless. Incorrigible, I thought. At least now my doctor will know what I'm up against.

I took Toby with me to get the sleep-test results. "Looks like my suspicion was on target, Brenda," my doctor said. "You stopped breathing fifteen times during the night. Your dog woke you every time."

Just like that, everything came into focus. No wonder poor Toby naps so much, I thought. He's worn out from trying to save my life! He was like those dogs I'd read about who have a remarkable talent. They can sense when a seizure or a cardiac episode is about to hit their owner and alert the person.

I looked at Toby, dozing beside my chair. I leaned over and stroked the soft reddish fur behind one of his ears. He opened his eyes and started to his feet. "No, you rest, Toby, you've earned it," I told him. "Will you give me another chance? I'll be as patient with you as you've been with me, I promise."

Toby licked my hand and lay down.

My doctor outfitted me with an oxygen tube to regulate my breathing while I sleep. Now Toby wakes me only if the tube slips off. It's pretty amazing how well we learned to work together once we both got enough rest. Before long Toby could do everything Farley had done. These days Toby and I train other dogs to help people with disabilities. He loves to demonstrate how to get a can of soda from the fridge, carry a bag and, of course, fetch slippers. My Toby is some service dog, all right. A real answer to prayer, one I didn't even know I needed, yet I couldn't live without.

# Three of a Kind

*Marilyn Sansom*

$\mathcal{S}$ix days in the hospital after open-heart surgery, and I was finally coming home. My neighbor drove me in her car up my street. A million thoughts clattered through my head. How was I going to manage? No more nurses and doctors monitoring me twenty-four hours a day. The stitches keeping my chest closed up caused pain if I tried to lie down. How would I get to sleep at night in an upright position? What would happen if I tripped or fell on the way to the kitchen or the bathroom?

Most of all, I worried about my cats, Schnookie, Ophelia and Simon. They depended on me for everything. A friend had been watching them while I was gone, but she couldn't take care of them forever. That was my job. I'd rescued each of them over the years.

The first one came to me on a cold September night. I pulled into the parking lot of a fast-food restaurant, planning to grab a quick dinner. Out of the corner of my eye I spotted a tiny ball of gray fur huddled near the Dumpsters. I walked over and saw it was a kitten, no more than ten weeks old, shivering. "Don't worry," I said softly. "I'll take you someplace warm." I lifted her up and zipped her into my jacket. There was no turning back. I took her home, got her treated at the vet and christened her Schnookie.

A few years later, on a Sunday morning in June, I was reading the paper when I stumbled upon the strangest classified ad I'd ever seen.

"Cat! Will trade for snake or money. Don't want anymore…" Was it a joke or something? That poor unwanted cat! I thought. I called the number, got the address and drove there with my cat carrier in the passenger seat. The second I stepped inside the house, I had a bad feeling. The owner introduced himself—he was a bagger at the local supermarket who had adopted the cat after her elderly owner had died. He led me into his back bedroom, where he said he kept the cat cooped up all day.

The first thing I saw was a huge tank holding a giant live snake. A python, the bagger explained. I was scared out of my wits. Cowering beneath a table on the other side of the room was the cat—Ophelia. She looked at me with sad green eyes. She was begging for help. This beautiful tabby had turned into a flea-bitten, nervous mess. I took her home, got her cleaned up and treated, and soon Ophelia and Schnookie were sleeping side by side on my sofa.

I wasn't planning on adopting yet another cat, but on a visit to the local shelter I came upon one of the most pitiful animals I had ever seen—a Siamese named Simon. Like Ophelia, his owner had also died. "If we don't find a home for him soon," the lady said, "we'll have to put him down." I let him out of the cage, and he brushed up against my legs. Then he took his two front paws and stood on the toe of my sneaker, staring up at me.

"Simon," I said, "you're coming home with me."

Each of the cats I had chosen, and yet, in a way, they had chosen me. Feeding them, talking to them, being with them gave me a real focus for my life. In fact, I became an advocate for cats whose owners died without making plans for them.

"Make sure your cats are mentioned in your will," I told other owners. "You don't want them to end up in a shelter."

Not that such a thing could happen to Schnookie, Ophelia and Simon—SOS, I called them. "I'll take good care of you," I assured them.

I'd answered an SOS from each of them. In fact, it felt like God had put me there to help them.

Then I had my own troubles. First, I started having problems catching my breath. I felt fatigued after a few steps. No energy. "You need heart surgery," my doctor told me.

"What about my cats?" I exclaimed. But I had no choice. I prayed they'd be fine until I came home.

That first day back from the hospital, I walked through the front door and there was Ophelia, lying at the end of the sofa with her head down on her front paws, looking like she'd lost her best friend. "Ophelia!" I called. She jumped off the sofa and ran toward me, meowing all the way. I started to bend down to pick her up, but the pain from the incision made me freeze. I can't even lift my cats, I thought.

I collapsed onto the living room sofa.

Ophelia nestled beside me. I heard the patter of little paws and saw Schnookie and Simon running in from the screened-in porch to join us. They hopped up on the sofa, their purrs vibrating through me.

That night I decided to sleep upright on the sofa. Schnookie jumped up on the sofa and walked along the back of it until she was right by my head. She reached a paw out and lightly touched my cheek. "Goodnight, Schnookie," I said.

Ophelia got up on a swivel rocking chair and curled up facing me, like she was keeping vigil.

Finally, Simon climbed up onto my lap and, careful to avoid my stitches, curled up and began to purr softly. Their warmth, their purring and their comfort quickly sent me off to dreamland.

In the middle of the night I woke up, needing to use the bathroom. I rose to my feet. The house was dark, and I was still dizzy and disoriented from the side effects of the surgery. No nurse to help me here, I thought. Then I felt Simon brush past my leg. He looked up at me, turned and began walking down the hall. I took a few steps forward. Then Simon stopped. Looked back. He's guiding me, I thought. Simon stayed with me all the way to the bathroom, then led me back to the sofa, where Schnookie and Ophelia were waiting to greet me. "You're my SOS team," I said to them.

It took me a year to recover from the heart surgery completely. But without my cats, it might have taken longer. Whenever I felt stressed and my heart rate would begin to soar, Schnookie, Ophelia and Simon seemed to appear out of thin air right by my side, to offer a snuggle.

Eventually, walking and cardio exercises brought my heart back to full strength. But it was my SOS team that helped me find the strength to heal.

When I first learned that I needed heart surgery, I was concerned about how I would care for my three cats. But God showed me that He had a plan all along. He made sure that His furry little angels— Schnookie, Ophelia and Simon—were right there to care for me.

# Then Came Shredder

*Barbara Aqua*

*I* opened the door to the Trents' house and was greeted, as usual, by Shredder, their Airedale. He bounded toward me, jumped up and put a paw on each shoulder. "Okay, boy," I said, rubbing the inside of his ears the way he liked. He moaned contentedly. Then he brought me the raggedy old stuffed monkey he liked to play fetch with. I tossed it down the hall a few times. "That's all for now," I told him. If Shredder had his way, I'd play with him all day. He was such a big dog, with energy to burn. But with so many things on my schedule—the PTA meeting, Girl Scouts, dinner, other houses to clean—I didn't have time.

I'd been cleaning for the Trents going on two years. I should have been used to Shredder being underfoot. After all, my husband, Dave, our two girls and I had a pair of high-energy Scottish terriers. That day I told Shredder to lie down on his pillow. "I've got to get to work now," I said.

I headed downstairs to vacuum the family room. Shredder settled on his carpet. *Probably can't wait till I'm done so we can play some more,* I though. *Too bad for him that I'm out of here soon as I'm finished.*

All of a sudden pain shot through my head. It was unlike anything I'd ever felt—ten times worse. Light exploded behind my eyes. The vacuum hose slipped out of my hand, and I fell to my knees. I knew someone who'd died from a brain aneurysm. Is that what's happening to me? I had to get help. Now. Before it was too late.

*Phone*, I thought. The nearest phone was in the kitchen. I tried to stand up, but couldn't. I have to get upstairs, I thought. The pain got worse. It felt like my head was going to explode. I managed to crawl to the foot of the steps. But I couldn't move anymore. I was helpless.

Through the pounding pain, I said a prayer. *God, I don't want this to be the end. I've got a husband and two kids who need me. I want to see them again. Please help.* I looked up. Shredder stared back at me from the top step, tail slightly thumping the floor. Did he think I was playing? "Come here," I whispered, trying to make my voice sound playful. He cocked his head and stared quizzically. "C'mon, boy," I said. Shredder padded down the steps and stood next to me. His tail stopped wagging. Did he sense something was wrong?

"Help me, Shredder," I said, grabbing his collar with my left hand. He climbed a step, then stopped. "Up!" I said. He looked back at me as if to say, "Is this right?" "Go," I whispered. Shredder started to drag me. My left arm went numb. I had to look at Shredder's collar to make sure I kept my grip. I reached with my right hand and managed to get hold of the banister. I strained to pull myself. Shredder tugged, and I made it up one step at a time.

I squeezed my eyes shut. Little explosions of light flashed across the inside of my eyelids. "Hurry, Shredder."

Shredder got me to the top of the steps. Then I started to crawl. Shredder grabbed my sleeve in his teeth. He pulled and tugged, helping me across the kitchen floor. Now I knew what that stuffed monkey must've felt like. Finally, the phone. *You're not going to make it. Call Dave.* I needed to tell him what had happened. I didn't want the Trents to have to deliver the bad news. I got the answering machine. The message I left must have scared him silly. "I'm at the Trents'. I think I'm having an aneurysm. I'm going to die. I just wanted to tell you I love you." Then I called 911.

Shredder sat down next to me. "Good boy." I wanted to rub his ear, but I couldn't. Still, he stayed right by my side.

The EMTs showed up in minutes. Shredder, who is friendly almost to a fault, jumped to his feet and started growling. "It's okay," I said.

He seemed to accept that they were here to help, and sat back down obediently, head cocked. "Any history of heart trouble?" one EMT asked.

"No," I told her. "It's my head. Pain."

"Looks like you've been without oxygen," she said. They strapped me to a gurney and rolled me out of the house. The last thing I recall is seeing Shredder.

Doctors discovered that a heart valve had gone into a spasm. It could have been caused by any number of things: a temporary blockage or a sudden severe migraine (which would explain the extreme pain in my head). They discharged me after four days, but I had another sixteen weeks of complete bed rest. All that lying around doing nothing nearly drove me crazy. Maybe I was a little bit like Shredder, always needing to be active. I kept worrying about all the PTA meetings I was missing, the dinners I couldn't fix, the houses I should have been cleaning.

Then one day my girls came into the room after school. "Mom, we're so glad you're here with us all the time!" one said. They told me about their day, then went off to do their homework. I thought about what they'd said. Maybe this was an opportunity to slow down and spend a little quality time with my family. *Okay, Lord. I get the message.*

Still, I couldn't wait to get back to the Trents' house. Not to clean. But to finish a game of fetch. Shredder had been waiting to play for too long.

# What Was Needed

*Lynn Seely*

*W*hat a hot August morning! Ted finished his coffee, carefully rinsed out his cup, then headed outside. Even at this early hour the heat and high humidity were stifling. Still, he wasn't about to break his routine. This was the one enjoyment he allowed himself, no matter what the weather was like. He was unaware his life was about to change forever.

Ted had always been a loner; a workaholic. Work was predictable; people were not. His neighbor's houses were not very close to his home and that suited him. In fact, he had never spoken to them during the five years he had lived here.

Only minutes after he was outside, his shirt started to cling to him in the hot, heavy air. Not a bit of breeze stirred anywhere. The sun was just beginning to send streaks of gold across the sky and birds were singing their morning songs, but he wasn't in the mood to appreciate anything. His mood matched the stifling air.

He needed to clear his mind of all the clutter that distracted him this morning. He concentrated on the rhythm of his stride. As he ran, he felt the tensions that defined him during the workday slowly dissolve.

Ted always ran on the same quiet country road. This dirt road meandered past beautiful meadows and forests. Then it would eventually bring him to a small bridge that crossed a stream, and finally, it would bring him to the lovely Susquehanna River. At that point the road turned sharply to the right and ran parallel to the river for miles. He never tired of the view of the river, or the jagged, stark, rocky cliffs that jutted straight up hundreds of feet high on the other side of the clear, shimmering water.

When he reached the river, he would be at his halfway point. It was then he would decide whether to continue following the road, which would eventually make a complete circular trip back to his home, or as he occasionally did, he might just turn around and retrace his steps.

Ted had almost reached the bridge when a pickup truck sped past him. It had come much too close, causing him to jump off the road. That was bad enough, but what really angered him was the truck's speed. It must have been doing at least fifty miles an hour on this narrow country road where the speed limit was only thirty!

The truck left a wake of thick dust that rose high in the air. It engulfed Ted and covered his damp body. Disgusted, he slowed to a walk and angrily pulled his shirt up over his nose and mouth as he waited for the dust to settle. He watched the truck slow down to a crawl as it crossed the bridge. He started running again, determined to catch up to the truck and give the driver a piece of his mind! But the truck sped up again and raced away, leaving another wall of thick dust to linger in the air.

Ted was certain he had seen something being thrown from the truck. He hated litter and took great offense at people who thought the world was their trash dump. When he arrived at the small wooden bridge he saw a burlap bag sitting half submerged in the shallow water below it. He could hear whimpering coming from the bag at first, then silence followed. He rushed down the steep bank, grabbed the bag and pulled it out of the water. He grimly realized what the bag likely contained. Once the bag was on dry ground, Ted untied the crude rope that secured it and opened the bag. A dripping wet puppy was inside as well as one very large rock. The bewildered brown puppy gazed up at him in fear and made not a sound.

Anger flooded him. Who could do such a thing? His anger was quickly replaced by concern for his tiny charge. Ted had not owned a dog since he was a kid, yet he knew at that moment that he would keep this puppy. He picked up the now-squirming puppy and was rewarded with happy licks with its tiny pink tongue. The little wagging tail told Ted how happy it was at being rescued.

Ted walked home with the small creature cradled in his arms. He spoke softly to him and planned how the rest of his morning would go. First a trip to the vet was in order, then a trip to the pet store for puppy food. He would delay going in to work for a few hours. Never mind that, he decided he'd take his long overdue vacation and spend some time with his new puppy.

Ted realized he would need to give the pup a name. Before he reached home he knew he had the perfect name for this brown puppy. Bubba! That was it. He would name him after his childhood dog. That dog had meant the world to him, and it felt right to have a living legacy. Yes, Bubba it would be!

Ted had never made time for anything in his life besides work and running, but Bubba changed all that. Bubba grew into a large, beautiful golden-colored dog. His friendly disposition invited smiles from all that met him. Ted ran with Bubba every morning and over time he got to know all of his neighbors on a first-name basis. They all seemed smitten with Bubba. He learned that Gracie, the old widow in the farmhouse nearest his home, had health issues and could no longer shovel her walk in the winter, so Ted began to do that for her. She would always invite Bubba and him into her warm house afterward. Ted enjoyed the tea and cookies she always offered, and of course the conversations about Bubba. He found out that Bubba reminded her of a dog she once had. That was something they had in common.

A family that lived farther down the road had a bunch of kids who adored Bubba. As soon as they saw Ted and Bubba coming down the road, the children would race out to pet the dog. After many hugs were bestowed on the gentle canine, the two would continue on. Ted got to know all of the neighbors and they became a family of sorts to him. All the neighbors were friendly now and they would wave to them as they'd pass and call out a greeting. Ted began to feel connected to others for the first time in adult life.

As the dog grew older, Ted even began to go to a few local running events and brought along Bubba. Most people loved the gentle, well-behaved Bubba. They often came over to pet him and ask questions. Ted found himself happily talking to people about his dog. Before Bubba, he would have avoided all contact and conversation. Ted was becoming friendly without even realizing it. And it was all because of Bubba.

Ted joined the local running club and started helping out at races. He always brought Bubba with him, of course. Bubba loved it. His golden-plumed tail gently waved the entire time he was at a race. He loved watching the crowd, but if you observed Bubba for any length of time, you couldn't help but notice that he was always aware of where Ted was. Bubba's gentle brown eyes would periodically search Ted's face and once reassured all was well with his master, would turn their attention back to whatever was going on around him.

"That dog really adores you, what's his name?" A young woman bent down to pet Bubba. She had dark hair held back with a blue sweatband. She had just finished the race that Ted was helping out at.

"My name is Lucy," she added. Twinkling brown eyes waited for Ted to respond. His friendly smile was an indicator that he was indeed a changed man.

"I'm Ted. This is Bubba."

With that simple introduction, his life would take yet another turn for the better. Soon he and the lovely Lucy were running together on a daily basis, always with Bubba right beside them. Ted and Lucy later married and over the years Bubba proved he was a loving and gentle guardian to their children. If he was watching over them, they knew their children would be safe.

Bubba is getting on in years now yet still insists on a morning run, no matter what the weather. He sits patiently by the front door with a leash in his mouth, tail wagging, eyes shining.

"We go a lot slower than we used to," Ted explained to me, "but we still go every morning."

I closed my notebook and thanked him for sharing this story with me before I added, "I'm so glad you were able to rescue Bubba that day."

Ted reached down and gently tugged on Bubba's ear as he said, "Me too, but you know, I think he rescued me that day too, didn't you, boy? That is what was needed, right Bubba?"

I couldn't have agreed more.

# The Boy Who Needed Alex

*Lori Shaw*

*M*y yellow lab, Alex, a certified therapy dog, tugged at her leash and trotted down the elementary school hallway, eager to get to the kids we'd been visiting the past couple of months. She stopped at our usual classroom. I straightened her red scarf and opened the door. But there were no kids. Just the teacher. *That's odd*, I thought.

For years, I'd prayed for the chance to raise a therapy dog, and Alex was a natural. A whip-smart, energetic pup, she breezed through obedience training. Her attentive amber eyes could melt the hardest of hearts. She became certified at just a year old. Deep in my heart, I knew Alex was meant to do good in the world. When one of her instructors told me about Dog Tales, a volunteer group that visits schools and libraries with therapy dogs, encouraging folks to read, it sounded perfect. Alex loved kids so I signed her up. Our assignment was the local elementary school. From our first visit, the kids bonded to Alex. Every time we came back, the students couldn't wait to sit and read with Alex.

But that day, with our regular class missing, I wondered if we could help at all. I worried about Alex. She needed to do her therapy work. "I'm so sorry," the teacher said. "I forgot to call you. The kids are out working on a project today."

Alex sat next to me and whined. "Could we visit another class?" I asked.

The teacher thought for a moment. "There *is* a class that would enjoy seeing..."

"Perfect!" I said. She led the way down the hall, and Alex and I followed. Then Alex stopped short in front of another door. "C'mon, girl," I said, tugging on her leash. But my normally obedient dog wouldn't budge. She wanted to, no, *had to*, enter this classroom. The teacher asked the class if they'd like to meet Alex. Then she waved us in. It was a small class, maybe ten kids. "Hi, everyone," I said. "This is Alex...."

Before I could finish, Alex made a beeline for a boy who was sitting on the carpet, his head down. She snuggled up to him and put her chin on his shoulder. The boy quietly put his arm around her.

I read a story to the kids. With each turn of the page, I caught a glimpse of the boy stroking Alex's coat. She never left his side. *That's funny*, I thought. Usually Alex makes her rounds and visits with all the kids. After we said our good-byes, the teacher walked over. "May I please speak to you in the hallway?"

"Of course," I said, following her.

"I know you have a schedule, but could Alex visit us each week too?"

"We'd love to," I said. Then I saw tears in her eyes. "Did I say something wrong?"

She shook her head and pointed to the little boy. "He's been depressed for months. We've tried everything, and we just can't break through to him. But it looks like Alex has."

Alex and I kept going back to that classroom. Each week that little boy brightened a bit more. Today he's a happy fifth grader, who still gets visits from Alex and me.

Who could've known Alex would make such a big difference in a child's life? But that's what happens sometimes, isn't it? We ask God to give us opportunities to help, and He leads us to where we're needed. Or rather, He led my dog.

# Devotion

## Doris Day

*I* have found that when you are deeply troubled, there are things you get from the silent devoted companionship of a dog that you can get from no other source.

# Gifts of
# Friendship

Animals are such agreeable friends—
They ask no questions,
They pass no criticisms. . . .

—George Eliot

# First Love

*Janna Graber*

The director has set up the shot, and the camera is ready. I've finished with makeup, and am ready to mount the sturdy quarter horse that will be my assistant in this scene of our in-flight travel show. The gelding shivers under my initial touch and sidesteps to the right. A soothing sound instinctively escapes my lips, and I run a gentle hand across his neck. The horse settles and I hop up, arranging the reins and getting settled.

"Can that chick ride?" I hear one of the ranch hands say. I smile and move the horse into position. It's been so long since I've ridden, but it's still a part of me, like learning to ride a bicycle. The realization feels good, but then a small ache wells up inside of me, a hole that seems unfilled. It's funny, even after all these years, how much I still miss her.

We were both fourteen years old when we met. I was a gangly eighth-grader who sported braces and tomboy ways. I was just entering life as a teenager, and boys and school and my changing body made me unsure of myself and my place in the world.

She was a small paint horse named Mazy. I don't know much about her earlier life, for she came into our lives quite unexpectedly. My dad had been down at the local feed store, buying grain for the herd of goats we kept on our small Colorado farm. While dad was paying for his grain, another man marched in and pinned a small notice on the announcement board. "Horse, tack and horse trailer for sale, $2,000."

It seemed too good to be true, so my dad enquired. The man, it turned out, was trying desperately to manage his out-of-control teenage daughter. If she ran away one more time, the man said, he had threatened to sell her horse. Well, she had done just that, and now the horse had to go.

It was my fourteenth birthday when my dad pulled up with a horse trailer, and Mazy daintily stepped out and into my life. All we knew was that she was "gentle" and also fourteen years old. Beyond that, she was a mystery.

I was instantly smitten. For the past year, I had been involved with a local riding club. For three dollars a session, I would rent a horse and ride with the drill team. Now, I would have my very own horse!

Perhaps she was used to teenage girls, for Mazy happily accepted me as her new owner. By accident I learned that she had been trained with clicking sounds. One click meant trot, two meant she would run. I barely had to prompt her to get her to ride as I wanted. And who would have guessed, but she could also "count" using her front right leg, and could rear up on command just like "Hi oh Silver!" I often impressed my friends with her tricks.

I spent hours on Mazy's back, sometimes riding in the saddle, sometimes bareback. Other times, I would simply hop on her with no tack at all, and lay on her back daydreaming while she grazed in our pasture.

In my riding team, she performed well. Small though she was, she was fast and responsive. When we rode in parades, I never had to worry that she would spook.

She had only one strange fear: yellow cars. Since our little farm had been surrounded by the suburbs, I often had to ride on the street, and I took great care to avoid yellow cars. We rode to open areas of land where we could run; other times we would ride along the bike paths.

A few times, I even took her through the Taco Bell drive-through (ah, the wisdom of a fourteen-year-old).

When I'd tire of our ride, I would simply turn her toward home, and Mazy always knew the way on her own.

That would come in very handy.

I first noticed that something was strange when I found the saddle sitting outside of the barn one afternoon. I questioned each of my seven brothers and sisters, but none of them claimed to have touched it. Since they had never shown any interest in our horse, I believed them.

A few days later, I found the bridle left out, and I knew something strange was going on. Someone else had been riding my horse! Indignant, I wrote a short letter that said: "If you would like to ride my horse, please come ask me first. Please do not ride my horse." I nailed it to the barn, and told my parents that someone had been riding Mazy. I wasn't sure if they thought I was crazy or not.

But when I came out after school the next day, the note was gone, and the saddle was left out again. I knew I wasn't dreaming it.

Two days later, we were awakened at 6 AM by the ring of our doorbell. "Is that your horse out front?" asked our neighbor. "She's been running back and forth, trying to get into your fence."

I looked outside and there was Mazy, frantically running back and forth. I called to her and she stopped, then I ran to her in my pajamas and bare feet. A broken rope, probably from baling twine, hung from her halter. I led her into the pasture, and spoke in soothing tones while I stroked her back and neck. She finally settled down and went to eat.

The police came and we eventually learned what had happened. Another teenage girl had seen Mazy and had started riding her when I was at school. One day she decided that she wanted Mazy for her own, and she'd stolen Mazy during the night. My horse had been tied to a fence at least three-quarters of a mile away, but she'd broken away and had come home on her own early in the morning.

To do so, Mazy had to cross a very busy street. Even more interesting was the fact that we had never ridden in the area the girl had taken her. How Mazy found her way home from there—and crossed such busy streets on her own—I will never know.

All I know is that I was overjoyed to see my horse, and I think she was happy to see me.

Mazy was my first love all through ninth and tenth grades, but then, as often happens, I dove head first into life as a teenager. I became a cheerleader, played softball and started dating boys. Oh, all those boys!

Poor Mazy. She often spent her days eating in the pasture or nuzzling with the horse next door over the fence. I'd ride her whenever my busy schedule allowed, but those times grew more infrequent. Then, I went away to college. My younger siblings rode Mazy occasionally, but none of them ever had the same connection with her that I had had. Eventually, my parents gave Mazy to a horse club that matched her with another family. And I was so busy with my new baby daughter and job, that I only had time for a brief visit to say good-bye. By then, Mazy and I were both twenty-four, and she was starting to move more slowly. A sob welled up in my throat as I stroked her and said good-bye. I hoped that she would enjoy her last years with another teenage girl.

Sometimes, you don't understand what you had until it's gone—and I know now what a treasure she was. As the years have passed, I've often thought of Mazy. I've never found another animal that I've loved so completely. Perhaps some people only find that once in a lifetime.

"Are you ready to ride?" the director calls, breaking me from my revelry.

"Yes!" I call back, getting set in the saddle. Mazy taught me many things—the joy that an animal can bring, the enjoyment of being outside, and the loyalty of a friend. But most of all, she taught me to ride.

A smile covers my face and I nod in memory of Mazy, and then ride into the shot.

# Loving Gracie

*Melinda Waxler*

$\mathcal{B}$ailey, my son Matt's pit bull mix, needed all my attention. My husband and I already had four dogs when we inherited Bailey after Matt died. In the months since, Bailey had only grown more and more depressed. She never played with the other dogs or barked, just lay in the living room, staring at the front door, waiting for Matt to come home. Whenever someone turned the knob, she'd raise her head hopefully, then drop it to the floor because it wasn't him. I knew the feeling. There were times I wanted to lie on the floor all day too. With Matt gone, my love for him sometimes felt like a burden. Still, loving Bailey kept me connected to Matt and helped to ease the heaviness in my heart. I wished I could say the same for Bailey.

"Come on, girl," I said, crouching beside her one morning. "Don't you want to go for a little walk?"

"Go on to work," my husband, Gary, said. "I'll spend some time with her before I leave." We'd done everything we could think of to make Bailey feel loved and at home. Nothing seemed to do it. I got in my car feeling hopeless. Lord, how do I show Bailey that life goes on? In many ways I was still trying to convince myself of the very same thing.

At work a friend was waiting for me with a surprise: a pug puppy with an eye problem who needed to be adopted right away. I looked at its wrinkled black face with one swollen eye. "Bailey has to be my focus now," I said, shaking my head firmly. "I'm sorry."

"Are you sure you can't take her?" my friend pleaded. "You were my last hope." People weren't used to hearing me say no to a dog, especially one this irresistible. I'd always had a soft spot for animals. Matt and I both. He would have taken the puppy. That, I knew.

"Well, I guess I could keep her while we find her a good home."

Gary was surprised when I walked in and gave him a peek at the little pug in her box. "I can explain," I said. Bailey lay in her spot by the door, listless like always. I carried the box into the living room. Gary followed.

"I hope I didn't do the wrong thing," I said, lifting the puppy from the box. "I'm calling her Gracie."

"I can see why you couldn't say no," said Gary. "Not to this face."

The minute I put Gracie down on the floor, she took off. Gary and I scurried after her. She hightailed it through the living room, jumped onto the coffee table, then the couch. She hopped to the recliner and I tried to grab her, but she wiggled out of my grasp and went slipping and sliding down the hall. "Gracie, watch out!" She tripped over Bailey in the foyer and raced into the kitchen. Our other dogs watched from the sidelines.

Bailey lifted her head and looked around for the source of the commotion.

"Sorry, girl," I said, kneeling beside her. So much for quiet introductions. "I'm sorry to bring another dog home. It's just for a little while. Can you be patient with her, Bailey?"

Bailey let out a weary sigh. Just then Gracie came tearing down the hallway again. "Gracie, don't bother Bailey," I commanded. Gracie paid me no mind. She stumbled right up to the bigger dog and touched noses with her.

Bailey gave Gracie a tentative sniff. I watched, holding my breath. Would she snap at the intruder? Lose interest the way she did with everything that wasn't Matt? Bailey thumped her tail on the floor once, twice. She took Gracie between her front paws and pressed her face to the puppy's squashy head.

"Thank you, Bailey," I said, rubbing her side. "I'll find Gracie a good home as fast as I can. I promise."

I took Gracie to the vet to have that eye checked. It was infected and had to be removed. The surgery went well, but we had to watch Gracie closely to make sure she didn't scratch off her bandages.

At home, Bailey lifted her head and kept it up while I got Gracie settled on a pillow. I went into the kitchen to fill her water bowl. When I returned Bailey had left her spot in the foyer and settled closer to Gracie in the living room.

Our Gracie didn't stay in bed for long. In the evening she jumped onto the coffee table again. The other dogs had gotten used to her and went about their business. But I noticed Bailey standing in the door-way, watching Gracie instead of the front door. "Looks like we finally got someone's attention," I said to Gary.

Gary wrestled with Gracie on the floor. Gracie dove for his hand and fell over. In a flash Bailey was there on the floor with them, standing stiffly and looking Gary in the eye like she wanted to give him a real scolding. "That's too rough," Bailey seemed to say. "You have to be gentle with Gracie."

Gracie took a break from roughhousing and went to her water dish. Bailey followed right behind her. Gracie lay on her pillow. Bailey lay next to her. Gracie tore through the house from one end to the other. Bailey ran right behind her.

When I brought Gracie home from the vet the day she got her bandages off, she went right to Bailey, who inspected her from head to toe and gave her face a good cleaning. "She's fine," I assured Bailey, stroking her head. "She just looks a little different from other pugs."

A couple of days later I came home to find Bailey sitting on the floor with something between her paws. An old Beanie Baby pug from my collection. "You've never chewed on anything before now, Bailey," I said, picking up the soggy toy. "What's gotten into you?"

I inspected the stuffed animal and showed it to Gary. We couldn't believe it. Bailey had chewed off one of the eyes!

Different from other pugs? Not as far as Bailey was concerned, and she let us know it. I had to watch what I said about Gracie in front of this loyal friend. I sat down on the floor and leaned my head on Bailey's. "You love Gracie, don't you, girl? Just like I love you."

Bailey still loved Matt. She still missed him terribly. Just like me. But we knew now that love is never a burden when you share it with someone who needs it most. With God's grace—and Gracie—Bailey and I would go on with our lives, making our house a good home. A good home for us all.

# A Pigeon Named Homer

### Jacqueline Donham

*I* sped down the last mile of Kentucky dirt road leading to the Nixes' driveway. Late again. Lord, he's going to bite my head off. I was working as a home health aide and had been assigned a new client, Dorothy Nix, just a few weeks earlier. She had a pixie haircut, twinkling eyes and an inevitable smile when she greeted me, even though she was in pain from her crippling arthritis. She was a joy to work with.

Her husband, Robert, a retired construction supervisor, was another story. "What took you so long to get here?" he growled on my first visit. "I thought I'd have to give Dorothy her bath myself." He followed me around the whole time, letting me know if I did anything that wasn't to his liking. "You're using the wrong dishes," he snapped. "That pillow isn't high enough!"

Dorothy always countered with a wink or an encouraging word. "Did you get a new haircut?" she asked me on my second visit. "You look so nice today." I hadn't gotten a haircut, but the remark was just what I'd needed on a day when I was feeling low. *She's such an angel*, I'd think. *How can she put up with someone so unpleasant?*

I pulled into the driveway of their small house. I could see Robert pacing in the big picture window. He's going to let me have it. Please, Lord, give me the patience to deal with this grouch.

Robert pulled the door open before I could ring the bell. Dorothy waved at me from her hospital bed in the middle of the living room.

"Sorry I'm late," I said. "How's everyone doing today?"

I braced myself for a sarcastic reply, but none came. Robert took my jacket and hung it up without a word. "I'm going to get to that work out back, Momma," he said and went into the yard.

"Mr. Nix seems awfully quiet today," I said, straightening up some things around Dorothy's bed.

"Yes, poor thing," said Dorothy. "He's been beside himself ever since he heard the news about Homer."

"Homer?" I tried to recall if that was the name of her grandson who had been sick with rheumatic fever. *No, that hadn't been his name.*

"Homer was Robert's pet pigeon. Several years ago he was supervising some rebuilding of the courthouse in Bardstown. A workman found a nest in the eaves with a baby pigeon in it. Robert brought it home and fed it from a medicine dropper. I didn't think the little thing would make it, but it did. When it got bigger, it would ride on Robert's shoulder while he worked in the yard. Those two were inseparable."

Dorothy might as well have been talking about a total stranger. It was hard to imagine her gruff husband mothering a baby bird. "So what happened to Homer?" I asked as I took Dorothy's vital signs.

"Just before you started working here our grandson came up from Tennessee to visit. He fell in love with Homer and begged Robert to let him take him home. Robert loves the boy so much he couldn't say no. Then yesterday we got a phone call. Homer flew away and they haven't been able to find him."

I glanced out the window into the backyard. Shoulders hunched and head bowed, Robert was loading a wheelbarrow with wood. I watched him for a minute, laboriously lifting log after log. A gust of wind blew off his cap and he went slowly after it. I didn't see an impatient and ill-tempered grouch. I saw an aging man with an ailing wife to care for and a sick grandson he loved so much that he gave up a beloved pet.

I'd prayed that God would help me through this visit. Now a prayer of a different kind came to mind. *God, Robert's life must be so difficult at times. Give him the simple strength to go on day to day. And help me not to be so quick to judge, to look beneath the gruff surface and see the kind heart within.*

I was putting fresh sheets on the bed when I heard footsteps on the outside stairs. Robert hurried through the door, cradling something in his hands. "See who just flew out of the sky!" he exclaimed. His leathery cheeks were wet with tears.

A plump gray bird fluttered its wings, then marched up the arm of Robert's jacket, cooing and pecking gently at his cheek. "Homer!" Dorothy exclaimed.

Robert knelt at Dorothy's side. In a shaft of sunlight, an iridescent rainbow of blue, green and purple feathers shimmered around the pigeon's neck. I stroked its silky head and the bird cooed at me. "Homer's taken to you," Robert said.

"I like him too," I replied. I liked the man holding him even more.

# Purrrrrfect

*Althea Kaye*

*I* lived on my own, and for months I'd been feeling lonely, so much so that I prayed about it. Finally I decided to get a cat. But I put off going to the pound. It wasn't just any cat I wanted. I was holding out for a friendly all-black tom with six toes. (I had heard six-toed cats have the gentlest dispositions.) I already had a name picked out: Aiisi.

One afternoon I was in my study working at my computer. I was on a tight deadline with a project. I distinctly heard a male voice say, "Go get a cat." Almost by reflex, I replied, "Okay, as soon as I finish this." The voice repeated, "Go get a cat." It was clear he meant now.

No more than forty-five minutes later I was at the pound. A young woman showed me the cats. I shook my head. None of them was Aiisi. Finally, the woman asked, "Do you have something specific in mind?"

"This might sound odd, but..." I told her everything on my list.

She gave me a strange look. "Follow me," she said. She led me to a cage in back. A black ball of fur was curled in the corner, purring like a well-tuned sports car. The woman opened the door and lifted him out. "Yup, he's a male," she said. I noticed his extra-large paws. Six toes!

"He's the one."

"He was brought in just forty-five minutes ago," the woman said. "Perfect timing."

And how!

# Gulliver Travels

*Roberta Sandler*

$\mathcal{M}$y pet beagle could do something none of my previous pet dogs could do.

He could ride in my car without getting motion sickness. That's why I named him Gulliver. Gulliver travels!

From the time he was a puppy, this adorable floppy-eared, tan-black-white canine was unhappy being left at home. He would give me a pathetically sad-eyed look as I walked out the front door. I would turn around as I headed for my driveway, and I'd see him peering at me through the living room window. Then, I'd hear his cry, a forlorn little howl that seemed to say, "Please take me with you."

At different times, a total of three dogs of different breeds had been my loving companion, but none of them did well in my car. They were nervous and they would soon make retching sounds and throw up in my car. Except for veterinary appointments, I left them at home.

Gulliver made me feel so guilty that, one day, I decided to risk it. As soon as I attached his leash to his collar, he knew he was going outside. As if that wasn't exciting enough for him, when he heard the jangle of my car keys in my hand, he must have associated the keys with my driving away in my car.

Gulliver put two and two together: the leash and the car keys, and he jumped for joy, sensing that he was about to go for a ride with me.

I was prepared. I placed an old blanket on the front passenger seat and after a few tries, Gulliver jumped high enough to land on the seat.

"This is a test, Flopsy," I told him, for I had originally chosen that name because of the way his ears flopped. "If you do well today, I'll let you ride with me more often."

I drove to the bank, wound my way up to the drive-in teller's window and inserted my bank deposit into the teller's tray. All the while, my curious little pup was eyeing the bank teller who smiled from behind her window.

"Oh how adorable," she said as she watched my dog climb interestedly onto my lap to get a better view of the teller. She asked me his name, his age and where I had gotten him.

In several years of using this bank, I had never said more than "Thank you" to the teller. I am painfully shy, and conversation with strangers makes me feel awkward and uncomfortable, yet while talking about my dog, I didn't falter and I didn't feel self-conscious.

A moment later, I reached into the tray to get my deposit receipt. Along with the receipt was a small bone-shaped dog biscuit. When I thanked the teller, I noticed two clear jars behind her window. One contained lollipops. The other contained dog treats.

I gave the treat to my dog and he contentedly nibbled on it, finding and eating every tiny piece that broke away and landed on the seat blanket.

When I returned home, I patted my beagle and said, "Congratulations, Flopsy. You proved that you can ride in my car without getting sick. I promise to take you on more travels."

That's when it hit me. I would give my dog a celebratory new name. "Okay, from now on your name is Gulliver," I told him. I assume he was pleased with the name change, because he jumped into my lap, stood as tall as his hind legs would allow, and he licked my face.

It was the first day of many days and many years in which Gulliver rode with me in my car. What I didn't realize, until much time had passed, was that Gulliver was changing me. He was making me more social and more confident.

I first realized it when I took Gulliver with me to a restaurant near the beach. The restaurant had outdoor tables where people were welcome to dine with their pets. It was my birthday and I was treating myself to lunch.

Gulliver wagged his tail at other patrons and at people who walked by. He was so cute that nobody could resist squatting down to pat his head. Inevitably, people would ask me about him, and as soon as I told them my dog's name, they wanted to know how I had chosen such a name.

This led to pleasant conversation with strangers. One woman was dining at the table next to mine, and she had her pet Schnauzer, Winston, with her. As Winston and Gulliver cautiously became acquainted with each other, the woman and I lapsed into a chat. I learned that she lived on the same street where I live. She was a widow. I guess I had been such a recluse that I hadn't met many of my neighbors.

"We live so close to each other, we could set up play dates between your dog and mine," she suggested. "Or we could walk our dogs together."

The woman was so lovely that I said, "That sounds like a great idea."

From that incident, Myra and I became friends. Occasionally, we would go out to dinner together, and sometimes we'd meet at her house or mine to play two-handed Canasta as Winston and Gulliver played and frolicked and chased each other through the house.

It was summertime and I wanted to visit my only long-time friend, Jane. Jane and I had grown up together and had gone from elementary school through high school together.

Through phone calls and letters, we had stayed in touch after I moved from Long Island to Florida. We had not seen each other in many years, and now she was inviting me to visit, and of course, by all means, bring Gulliver. Jane was a dog-lover and had recently had to put her beloved boxer to sleep.

I didn't want to put Gulliver through the ordeal of a plane trip, so I decided to drive to Long Island. En route, I'd stay overnight at a motel that permitted pets.

There we were, Gulliver and I, driving on Interstate 95 and listening to audiobooks and having conversations. Well, I was the one doing the talking; Gulliver was the one who absorbed my words. Drive-up windows of fast food chains meant that I didn't have to leave Gulliver alone in my car while I ate meals.

It was all so convenient, and I loved having my dog's companionship. He seemed so content being able to enjoy this long ride with me. He also made the trip interesting for me.

Along the length of I-95, there are abundant rest stops with areas where travelers can walk their dogs. Many times, I'd fall into brief conversation with other travelers walking their dogs. They were from the Carolinas and Virginia and other coastal states, and we all had something in common—loving and loved dogs who were our traveling companions. We'd laughingly compare notes about our dogs and their antics, and about where we were headed and why.

From that first long-distance journey came another journey by car the following summer, and yet another road trip the summer after that. Without fail, Gulliver would unwittingly become the catalyst for my meeting people and chatting with them.

Gulliver changed me. His enthusiasm and friendliness were contagious.

He made me unafraid to meet people and to invite polite conversation. I like to think he gave me the courage to join a club, to enroll in a course at my local college and to be less introverted and more outgoing.

It's strange to think that a dog could have such power and influence, and yet, I'm proof that Gulliver possessed these traits. Gulliver passed away, but I still take road trips, I still initiate conversations and I still think lovingly of the special little dog who could travel.

# Dixie's Kitten

*Anne Watkins*

$\mathcal{A}$n English setter, Dixie was a pretty dog who wore a white coat that was decorated with black and brown markings. In her younger days, she had spent many happy hours in the fields and woods hunting quail. She had the reputation of being a fine bird dog and her puppies were much sought after. They were trained to hunt under Dixie's watchful eye, and each litter was claimed before the pups were even weaned.

But now Dixie was so ancient that she spent most of her time lying in the sun beside her doghouse, soaking up the warmth of the rays. There was a full water bucket and brimming food dish within easy reach, and her house was lined with clean, fragrant hay. There were times when her old bones ached and pained her, and she would groan as she stood up to move to another patch of sunlight. But sometimes there were wonderful days when somebody brought by a young bird dog pup, and a spark would leap to her tired eyes. She adored puppies and would forget her age for a little while as she romped with the young dogs.

"No more puppies for you, old girl," I told her one day, stopping to pat her head and comb my fingers through her silky hair. She wagged her tail and looked toward the pup being admired in the front yard. Then, with a soft whine, she eased her aching body into a more comfortable position and dropped her chin to her paws. Her eyes fastened on the younger dog, she seemed lost in thought. Probably dreaming about the days when she was running through the fields teaching her own little ones to sniff out quail, I decided. I gave her one last scratch behind the ears and went into the house.

Lately, Dixie had seemed so lonely. I remembered the family of duck that used to cross the road in front of our house every evening to share her dish of dog food. Not once had Dixie growled or snapped at the ducks, and sometimes she would even move aside so they could have better access to her food. Visiting cats were always welcome to share her meals, and it wasn't unusual at all to find her with her nose in the same bowl with several ducks, cats and whatever stray dog may have wandered up. Dixie was a gentle, social soul, and nowadays there just didn't seem to be as many guests dropping by to have dinner with her.

One day there was a knock at my door. I opened it to find my next-door neighbor, Keith, standing there, a concerned look on his face. "Have you seen my kitten?" he asked. "He's missing."

I had played with the kitten a few days earlier. It was cute, fluffy little thing, not much bigger than a minute, and I knew Keith was right to be concerned. A tiny, lost cat would be no match for any sort of predatory animal in our rural area.

I told him I hadn't seen him, but that if I spotted him, I would give him a call. He thanked me, sadness shadowing his face. "He's so little," he explained as he headed off for the next house. "I'm afraid if I don't find him soon, something bad will happen to him."

Later that afternoon I carried a pan of dog food out to Dixie. She was in her house and I could hear her tail thumping out a greeting as I poured the food into her bowl. I fetched the water hose and filled her bucket, then called her out to eat. She emerged slowly and then painfully, carefully stretched. As I reached down to pat her head, a tiny gray kitten stepped out of the dark doghouse and twined itself around Dixie's legs.

"What have you got there, girl?" I exclaimed. Dixie glanced down at the kitten, then looked back up at me with a gleam in her eye. Her tail wagged harder. "Come here, kitty," I said and reached for it. Dixie gently pushed my hand aside with her nose and nudged the kitten back inside the doghouse. Sitting down in front of the door, she blocked the kitten's exit and I could hear it meowing inside. This had to be my neighbor's lost kitten. It must have wandered through the thicket of bushes between our houses and into Dixie's doghouse.

"Crazy dog," I muttered. Dixie wagged her agreement, but didn't budge from in front of the door. She waited until I was a safe distance away before she stood up and began nibbling at the pile of food. I phoned Keith.

"I think I've found your kitten," I told him. I could hear the relief in his voice, then the laughter as I told him that Dixie had been hiding it out. Promising to come over in the morning to collect the runaway cat, he hung up after thanking me again.

Keith showed up bright and early the next day, eager to look at the kitten. "Yep, that's my cat!" he said as the little gray furball stepped out of the doghouse. Dixie backed away from us and nosed the kitten toward the house. Gratefully, Keith reached for the cat. To our surprise, Dixie snarled at him.

Shocked, I scolded her. Keith reached for the kitten again, and this time Dixie bared her teeth. "Let me try," I said. I reached for the kitten but Dixie shoved it inside the doghouse, then followed it in and flopped down, blocking the tiny cat from us with her body. Nobody was going to take her kitten!

"Huh," Keith said. The kitten purred inside the house and rubbed itself against Dixie's face. She licked its fur and glared out at us. It was plain that she had adopted the little cat and planned to keep it. "Huh," I said. At the moment, it seemed the only thing to say.

"Well, it looks like the kitten's happy," Keith said after a few minutes. The little gray cat had curled up between Dixie's front paws and was grooming itself intently. Every once in a while it stopped to lick Dixie's face. Kitten and dog seemed perfectly content. Keith sighed, "I guess she can keep the kitten, if she wants it that bad."

So Keith went home without his cat, and my old bird dog got to keep her little foundling. Since there were no more puppies in her future, Dixie had made do with the next best thing. That old dog raised the gray kitten and when it become a full-grown cat, he wandered away one day to do whatever things tom cats do. And Dixie lived out the rest of her days contentedly basking in the sun, dreaming of kittens and puppies and romping in the fields.

# Strange Bedfellows

*Marilyn A. Gelman*

*I* am sixty-two years old and allergic to dogs. I never owned a dog before, much less a puppy. Yet these nights I share my lumpy mattress with a cockapoo named Buffy.

It didn't start out that way. She slept in her crate in the kitchen until an old diesel Mercedes caught fire in a driveway six feet from my leaky windows. Fumes permeated our small house. When I returned from treatment for smoke inhalation, I brought Buffy into my room to sleep; the air was slightly better there. Since then, she howls if she is not in bed with me. To tell the truth, I miss her too.

In a misguided effort to separate dog and woman, I created a special place for her at the foot of my bed, piling items for her comfort as follows: folded top sheet, waterproof pad, late son's old art project towel, and slightly chewed fleece bedding she had slept under in her crate. A smelly piece of braided yarn, a favorite toy, decorates her bed on a bed. Buffy has taken over half the remaining bed, choosing to sleep parallel to, not atop, her special setup. I wrap myself around the remaining real estate like a disproportioned capital L. the top half of my body is positioned at a sharp angle from the bottom half, and important parts of me rest on a wayward spring in the mattress. *If the spring pokes me,* I wonder, *will I need a tetanus shot?*

People who live with dogs say their appeal is the unconditional love dogs give. But to me, the opposite is true. My dog's special appeal is her willingness to accept love from me.

I have always enjoyed simple physical intimacies; a firm handshake, a casual touch on the shoulder, a quick hug from a friend. These intimacies were taken from me when a BMW crashed into my life. No one touched me except doctors. As I became isolated at home, old friends faded away, and I had no chance to make new ones. There were no full body hugs, strokes or casual embraces given or gotten. No one welcomed my caresses.

Now I have a pup who sits on my lap on occasion. I can touch her, pet her and groom her. She rests at my feet so that I cannot move without her knowledge. She makes me burst out laughing. It feels so good.

Buffy is a social butterfly. My injuries had made me a hermit. Now, I return waves and smiles from passersby when we sit on the front porch. They're smiling and waving at her, but she takes me with her into the social world I had missed for so long.

To the amusement of folks around here, Buffy has two strollers. They are for my benefit, not hers, I explain in vain. Balance problems have kept me close to home; stroller handles are the right height to hang onto for support. So I pile the Buffy into a stroller and take off for widening circles around the block.

Sometimes it's a little too chilly for a dog just to sit in a stroller, so I put a red, quilted, fleece-lined jacket on her or maybe a pink turtleneck sweater with cable stitching and sequins.

"Fine dress," laughs the neighbor down the block, new to English, but able to turn a phrase or two.

"Oh, so she can walk," he said when he saw Buffy on a leash. His wife explains that the dog is like a family member to me, and I dispute her.

But how can I make my case while wearing an outfit that matches my dog's?

I had some misgivings about getting a puppy, but my doctor encouraged me to try. "Everything is harder for you," the doctor said, "and this will be too. But just think of the possible benefit." He knew that social isolation was one of the most difficult aspects of my injury and that caring for a puppy could be just the thing to ease me back into humanity. And so I bit.

I wanted to name the pup Beautyrest, because I used my mattress money for her. The breeder dissuaded me, saying, "Imagine calling your dog. Your neighbors will think you are calling your mattress." She also vetoed Gussie as old-fashioned, even though both our grandmothers shared the name and made great stuffed cabbage. So my first-generation mix of cocker spaniel and poodle became Buffy—Buffarina Ballerina, in full.

Over the past decade of my younger son's death—two car crashes, cancer and diabetes—I have felt my heart break. I hadn't known people could feel hearts breaking over time, pieces detaching from the whole and floating down to who-knows-where. Amazingly, Buffy is making my heart whole again.

Sometimes I just stare at her while she sleeps, trying to be quiet so as not to wake her. I search for the mechanism she uses to reattach the pieces of my heart. I like to think she works with fuzzy multicolored yarn, threaded through a wide-eyed needle, so much like the yarn and needle my mother used to finish afghans she made for anyone with a chill. Despite my search, I cannot find the instrument. But my heart heals.

Recently, I stirred at night and became indignant when I felt Buffy too near to me. As close as we were together, she was clearly far out of bounds. I opened my eyes to move her, to whisper "place," and to correct her for her faux pas. Much to my surprise, I found that Buffy was where she belonged. I was the one who had migrated to intimacy.

# Then Came Ralph

### Kathleen Muldoon

_I_ never believed people who said you could love a pet as much as a family member. Not me. I didn't have any pets growing up, and I didn't want any now.

Especially now. I had just started a new job in a new town—San Antonio, Texas—doing the billing for a psychology practice. My boss was nice enough and the job was decent, but so far I felt unsettled. I'd moved down here from Pittsburgh because I was tired of the cold and because three good friends of mine and their families had made the same move a few years before and loved it.

But all three families moved away soon after I arrived. I was alone in a strange city. I dreaded coming home to my sparsely furnished apartment. I watched TV in my easy chair and prayed, _God, please send me some friends._

One day at work I got a call from a woman named Marcia, a friend of my boss. "Since you're new in town," she said, "I thought you might be just the person to help with a stray kitty."

Stray kitty? I almost hung up on her. But I had to be nice.

"He's living on the roof of my carport," she went on. "I can't take him inside because I've got dogs. He really needs a home—even if it's only for a short time."

The "okay" came out of my mouth before I could stop it. I gave Marcia my address and agreed that I would see her the next afternoon—Saturday—at my apartment. Why I agreed to it I'll never know. I suppose I was clinging to the idea of a "short time." That was my escape clause, anyway.

Mid-afternoon the next day there was a knock on my door. "You must be Kathleen," said a woman with a chipper smile, cradling a grocery bag in one arm and carrying a big blue animal carrier with the other. "I'm Marcia. You don't know how grateful I am to you! Here's some kibble and a kitty-litter tray to get you started. Now, don't you worry. We'll try it out for a week and see how things go. I'm sure he'll settle down and feel right at home before you know it."

Marcia put the carrier on the floor and opened the little front door. A ragged black cat emerged and proceeded to shoot around my apartment like a balloon someone had let the air out of.

"Thanks again!" chirped Marcia. Then, with one smooth move, she closed the door to the carrier, swept it up and out the door she went.

I sank into my easy chair to watch the cat. He finally slowed down and trotted nervously through my three small rooms. Then he plunked himself down in the middle of the floor and commenced licking his coat. Just as abruptly, he got to his feet and pounced into my lap. He took a few quick turns and, as if it were the most natural thing in the world, curled up and shut his eyes.

I sat there for a few minutes, hands at my sides, not quite knowing what to do, watching as the cat's breathing became more regular. Finally, he began to purr. A gentle, wonderfully contented sound. But just to be careful, I decided I wouldn't give him a name so that I wouldn't get too attached.

That was the end of my quiet little life in my quiet little apartment. Who knew cats were such crazy creatures? Calm one moment, a ball of energy the next. He pushed open doors that I wanted closed, pushed closed ones that I wanted open. He pounced at the TV set, pulled my bathroom towels off their hangers and flushed out dust bunnies from under the refrigerator. But the biggest change in my lifestyle was this: I couldn't sit or lie down without instantly turning into a piece of cat furniture.

Each morning, the cat sat by the door and bid me a silent good-bye, eyes following me out the door, as I headed out to work. He was waiting at the same spot in the evening, greeting me with an impatient meow.

"I see. Anxious for your feeding, aren't you?" I would say and pour out a big bowl of kibble for him.

No doubt the cat enjoyed his meals. That was for sure. But I think that he enjoyed me too, curling up in my lap and purring away.

"All right," I said on day four, "maybe you should have a name."

The cat looked at me and blinked.

"You're a run-of-the-mill black cat," I said. "So don't expect me to be giving you some fancy name. It's going to be something everyday, like Sam or Ralph . . . ." The cat let out a quick meow. Ralph it was.

Ralph's "trial week" came and went without either of us marking the day. I can't say that Marcia called to remind us of it either.

Before I knew it, I wasn't just talking to Ralph now and then, but giving him full reports on my day. It was talk therapy—just like the therapists at my job dispensed. Only Ralph charged a whole lot less. A dish of kibble and a lap to curl up in was all he asked.

"You're such a good therapist," I said to him one day, "that I ought to call you Doctor Ralph."

So Ralph got a new nickname. Sometimes I even called him El Doctor, since so many of the patients at the place where I work were Spanish-speaking. I couldn't help myself. I had become one of those animal nuts who treat their pets like people! Was it just because I was lonely? No, no. This was different. This was love.

Day by day, the news I gave Ralph was more cheery.

"So, you have a cat?" a woman asked me in the laundry room one day. "I often see him in your window. He's beautiful. I'm Veronica, by the way. I'm new to San Antonio."

"So am I!" I said. Before long, Veronica and I were talking all the time. She introduced me to a neighborhood church where I met more people. Doctor Ralph was still my best friend in San Antonio, but he was no longer my only one.

Did I say friend? Yes, Doctor Ralph had indeed become just that. But God had done more than give me a friend. In fact, Ralph was just like family.

# Unlikely Friends

## Lynn Seely

*T*he drought was over. Relief had finally come to the parched forests and the wild animals that live in the mountains. The light rain was perfect to run in and I was relishing being outside. I wondered if I'd be able to catch another glimpse of the fawn and her very unusual companion.

The dirt road I was on had been dusty to run on lately, but this morning it was a cool, inviting brown path where raindrops were gently skydiving into new puddles. The refreshing shower washed the dust off everything and in doing so created new visions of familiar scenery. Trees hung down, fresh and green, bent slightly as droplets clung to every leaf. It looked as if tiny jewels were decorating everything in sight.

The road took me past crystal clear creeks that flowed over ancient rocks; the boulders smoothed slick through time, and then on to immense, ancient trees whose branches embraced and formed a tunnel overhead. They seemed to murmur in the soft rain as I passed beneath them. They embodied dignity and calmness and were living proof that even though storms may come, it is possible to survive most of them. This summer, as the sun beat down upon me, they offered me a cool haven of shade. Today they offered me a serene cathedral—a tunnel of tranquility to run through.

The rain ended just as I arrived at the place where I was going to stop. I slowed to a walk, and took in the beauty before me. Tall trees scented the air with the heavy fragrance of pine, and the meadow where the fawn usually appeared was wet and sparkled in the dim morning light. In the distance I could see a smoky mist rising from a small lake. Beyond that, a distant mountain glistened, clean and pristine, the mantle of dust gone. I stepped off the road and made my way over to a fallen log. The ground was carpeted with emerald green moss; living velvet that made everything it draped appear soft and inviting. Moss covered the very bottom of the log, while the top was bare wood. It made a perfect seat at my favorite resting place. As I sat down, I wondered if the fawn would appear this morning.

While I waited, birds serenaded me with their morning songs and invited me to experience their enthusiastic joy. I watched some of them use the puddles in the road to bath in. They seemed relieved that the long drought was over. I noticed fresh tracks in the cow-brown earth. Some were strange looking tracks that I could only speculate about what had made them. A hawk soared low overhead, but it had been so silent and disappeared so quickly into the gray mist I wondered if I had imagined it.

I had not seen any deer this morning, but when I had encountered them before, they always seemed astonished at my presence. I have laughed out loud at the expression on their faces. They are not afraid of me, but they do seem amazed that a lumbering human would do such a thing as run! They often show me what true grace is as they wheel about and silently bound up a mountainside or across a grassy meadow.

I was almost ready to return home when I saw her. The little fawn was walking carefully, ears twitching for any sound that could mean danger. I froze, not wanting to startle her. She had beautiful brown eyes, and dappled white spots still covered her tawny coat. She was too young to be without her mother, yet it was clear she was.

Had her mother been here, she would have spotted me easily, as the other deer always had. But because the fawn was very young and inexperienced she had not yet learned the lessons she needed to. As delighted as I was to see her, I worried about her.

Suddenly her friend appeared. I wondered if he would see me and then warn the fawn as it had before. Sure enough, the next instant, a piercing squawk filled the air again and again. The fawn's friend happens to be a large black crow! I had seen the crow with the fawn on three occasions. And now, as before, it was warning her. The fawn stood alert for a moment, her ears twitching nervously—searching for the danger. It still did not see me. The crow then came closer to me and squawked a louder warning. The fawn turned toward the crow, saw me and wheeled about, her white tail a flag of alarm. In an instant she was gone. The crow stayed only a few moments longer, squawking loudly before it became silent. It then flew off in the direction the fawn had bounded away in. The first time I had witnessed this happen, I thought perhaps it was just by chance that the fawn had reacted to the crow. But now I was convinced the crow and fawn were friends. I smiled. The fawn wasn't alone after all. She had a friend. Indeed—though I had to admit it was a strange friend for a fawn to have—the crow was a good friend nonetheless.

I have never heard of such a friendship and I can only guess how it came to be. However, I do remember a lone crow I had noticed the year before. For some reason it seemed to be an outcast from the flock of crows that frequented the area. In fact, I saw them chase him away and I remember feeling sorry that he was not allowed to be with them. I can't say for certain that this was the same crow, but I suspected it could be. Perhaps the crow was very lonely and had somehow connected with the little motherless fawn. Perhaps the crow was a female and was trying to mother the fawn. Speculation aside, the fact was these two had somehow struck up a special friendship.

It was time for me to leave, and I decided to return home a different way than I had come. When I was about halfway home I reached the top of a very steep hill. I paused for a while and gazed out at the vast miles of creation stretched before me. I took a few minutes to absorb the beauty of it all. A mountain range lay in the distance, shrouded in swirling mist. The early morning sun was sending streamers of golden light dancing across the eastern slopes of the mountain nearest me as well as across the neatly cropped cornfields that stood silent and empty.

Well, almost empty. There in the cornfield, walking side by side, were the little fawn and the crow. Although the corn had been harvested there were pieces of it on the ground. The little fawn and the crow were making their way across the field, eating. Each seemed content in the company of the other; with their best friend.

# Get Well, Kate

## Phyllis Hobe

*E*ven before I took Kate, my big, beautiful German shepherd, to the veterinarian, I knew she was in great trouble. She had been limping. At first, I thought she'd hurt her leg playing ball. But the limp came and went, and on rainy days Kate could barely get around.

"She has dysplasia in her left hip," Dr. Guiliford said, shaking his head sadly. He fastened a large X-ray to a light screen. "There," he said, pointing to the bone where the top of the leg bone fitted in the hip joint. "You can see why she's in pain every time she takes a step."

The top of the leg bone, which should have been round and smooth, was knobby. Calcium deposits had made it larger than it should have been. Instead of moving comfortably in the hip joint, the leg bone was grinding against it. I winced, imagining how it must hurt. Yet Kate had never complained. She was always eager for a hike, a swim or a ball game. It was as if she didn't want to worry me. She's that kind of dog.

But I *was* worried. Terribly. *Dysplasia* is an ugly word to dog owners; it's common in large dogs. I knew of so many dogs whose lives had been cut short by it—and dog owners whose eyes filled with tears as they recalled putting a dog to sleep to end its suffering.

"But Kate's only four years old!" I protested.

"It happens to young dogs too," Dr. Guiliford said.

To understand how I felt, you have to know what Kate means to me. She's not a pet; she's a companion. I'm a writer and I live alone. As I move through my house, Kate is always with me. When I'm at my desk, she's under it. I'm not a natural athlete, but she's taught me what a treat the outdoors can be. She likes nothing better than welcoming friends to our home—and when my friends invite me to dinner, they almost always invite her too. My neighbors' children come over to play with her. She also makes it possible for me to live in the country—which is important for me—without feeling lonely or afraid.

I was so sickened by the possibility of losing Kate that it was hard for me to understand what Dr. Guiliford was saying. He was telling me about a new surgical procedure that would eliminate the pain. It's called arthroplasty, he said. He could refer me to an excellent orthopedic veterinary surgeon. The degree of Kate's recovery, however, would depend on a long period of post-operative therapy. "That's where you come in," he explained. "That'll be your job. But there's a good chance that Kate can return to an active, happy life."

"A good chance" wasn't good enough. I wanted a guarantee. And I wanted it right away, without putting Kate through surgery. You can't tell a dog, "You're going to be all right in a couple of months." Animals only understand the here and now, so any form of hospitalization confuses and frightens them.

I panicked. All the way home I prayed, "Please, Lord, heal my crippled dog." I believed so passionately that He could do it that for the next few days I watched closely for signs that Kate's limp was disappearing. I honestly expected a sudden, dramatic recovery—I thought that was the way God would do it.

Then I realized I had no right to tell God how to do anything. "I know nothing about healing, Lord. I'll leave that to You. I just want Kate to get well and I'll do whatever You think is best. We all will." Kate put her head in my lap, a signal for me to scratch her ears. Her limp was worse. I made an appointment with Dr. Lynne Maletz, the orthopedic veterinary surgeon recommended by Dr. Guiliford to do the operation.

"She a good candidate for arthroplasty," Dr. Maletz said after examining Kate and the X-ray. "Your job after the surgery will be to walk Kate very slowly on a short leash several times a day. Gradually she'll begin to use the leg we worked on."

Two days later Kate was home, still a bit groggy from the anesthesia. Her entire left leg was shaved down to the skin, and a stitched, eight-inch incision glared from her hip. She got around on three legs, the fourth swinging loosely and not touching the ground.

She was weak and slept a lot. She was thin, too, and I couldn't get her to eat. Even ground beef didn't appeal to her, and day by day she got weaker. One evening when my step-father called to find out how she was, I broke down, "I'm scared, Dad," I wept. "She can barely stand up—what'll I do when she can't?"

"Scrambled eggs," my dad said. "She loves scrambled eggs! Have you tried that?"

"No—but I will!"

I scrambled two eggs and let them cool. Then I crouched down next to Kate's bed, propped her up against me, and brought the bowl to her mouth. Nothing. I held the bowl there, waiting for her dry nose to catch the scent of the food. Suddenly, she raised her head and plunged her snout into the bowl. The eggs disappeared. I made, and she ate, three more portions that night. The next day I did what my mother would have done for me: I made her a pot of chicken soup and she ate it all. The day after that, she was back on her regular diet and starting to fill out.

Now it was time for me to start Kate's walking therapy. "There'll be no further possibility of dysplasia because we removed the damaged top of the leg bone," Dr. Maletz had explained. "We've made her a new hip socket out of muscle and cartilage so that'll feel strange to her for a while. Figure on six to eight weeks before she puts full weight on that leg."

Two weeks went by, but instead of beginning to use the dangling leg, Kate was getting around fairly well on three legs. She refused to put weight on the fourth. The muscles in the dangling leg were starting to atrophy.

I knew what the problem was. German shepherds are known for intelligence; during our slow walks Kate had time to figure out how to avoid putting her left hind foot on the ground. Off the leash she scampered around like a kangaroo, willing to make the best of what she had. But that left leg was getting skinny, and it was always cold as ice.

I panicked again. Was there to be no healing? Was the operation a success and the patient still crippled? Kate's recovery was in my hands now, and I didn't know what to do. "Help me, Lord!" I prayed, leading Kate in our slow walk that was getting us nowhere.

Then I remembered Bill McGlinchey, the trainer who taught me how to handle my large, rambunctious, powerful dog when she was younger. He knew so much about animal anatomy and behavior; maybe he could come up with a solution.

He did. "Remember what I told you in our first lesson?" he said. "You have to work her fast; don't give her time to think. Try walking her at a fast trot. Let her get tired from using only one hind leg. Then, when she puts the other foot down, give her a lot of encouragement. Try some sharp right and left turns too."

It was a cold day, but we went out and put Bill's advice to work. I hated to force Kate to run so hard, and she tired quickly. But she looked up at me, her tongue hanging out of the side of her mouth, and I saw trust in her eyes. We kept running until my lungs were numbed by the cold air. And then I saw it. The left hind foot came down. Just a little, the toes scraping the road surface.

"Thank you, Lord!" I whispered. And as I did, I realized that healing is far more complicated than I expected it to be. It isn't God stepping into our world and wiping out all our problems with a wave of His mighty hand. It is God bringing together enough of us to solve our problems with the talents, the insights, the dedication, patience and determination that He has already given to us. It is God's love motivating us to do what we didn't know we could do, to remember what we thought we had forgotten, to call upon others for the skills we ourselves don't possess.

Kate is fully recovered now and as active as ever. She'll always walk with a slight limp because one hind leg is shorter than the other, but you wouldn't notice it unless I told you. And she has no pain—because God brought together everything she needed to get well: the talents and training of her doctors, my stepfather's good memory, the training with Bill McGlinchey long before Kate ever began to limp, and, in spite of my lopsided way of expressing it, my belief in Christ's compassion.

Now, I call that a healing.

# Cats Make Us Feel Good

*Roger Caras*

*C*ats make one of the most satisfying sounds in the world: They purr. Almost all cats make us feel good about ourselves because they let us know they feel good about us, about themselves and about our relationship with them. A purring cat is a form of high praise, like a gold star on a test paper. It is reinforcement we would all like to believe about ourselves—that we are nice.

# Amazing Animals

*If I spent enough time
with the tiniest creature—
even a caterpillar—
I would never have to
prepare a sermon. So full of
God is every creature.*

—Meister Eckhart

# The Shedding

## Lonnie Hull DuPont

$\mathcal{M}$y husband and I live with our two housecats in a small house in the Michigan countryside. We love and enjoy our cats, but we also enjoy the wildlife that comes to our couple of acres. Our yard and the woods and swamp next to it are thoroughfares for turtles, foxes, coyotes, wild turkeys and skunks. Plus songbirds, hawks, cranes, great blue herons—they all fly in to our place.

And deer. I never tire of seeing them. They wander through the yard from tree line to tree line. They drink water from the pond and eat apples from the trees. They come singly or in pairs or in small herds. Even though I'm indoors, I stay quiet when they're in the yard and move slowly in the house so that my movement in our many windows doesn't spook them.

Each year I come to recognize some of the does and their offspring. Often there are twins, even triplets. Just beyond my back deck, I've seen spotted fawns chase each other in circles, kick up their heels, chest-butt one another, and even stand on their hind legs to try to snag an apple from a tree.

I rarely see bucks, at least not bucks that have their antlers. Once, I did watch a young antlered buck place himself between my deck and several does when he caught my movement through the window. He stomped his foot and huffed at me. Then the spooked herd turned and ran into the trees and the wetlands beyond, splashing through the swamp water—I could hear them trumpeting alarms to one another. It thrills me every time I see and hear such things.

One early morning in mid-March, my husband and I were starting our work days. My husband was shaving, getting ready to leave the house. I work at home, so I had just settled down to the computer with my coffee when I saw movement outside the slider door to the deck. A small herd of deer meandered through the back yard, grazing. I counted eight of them, and I saw that one had a rack of antlers, something I rarely see in my yard. I counted the points on his rack—eight— and noted that it was a rather small rack for so many points.

I quietly called to my husband to look out the bathroom window at the eight-point buck and his seven girlfriends. He too remarked that it was a small rack for so many points. The deer moved slowly through the yard and into the trees. I knew I'd see them again since herds tend to roam around the same real estate each year.

St. Patrick's Day was a couple days later, and I woke up feeling kind of down that morning. I wasn't sure why. I made my coffee, fed the cats, got my husband out the door, then curled up in my reading chair for some quiet time. I considered my sadness and what was causing it. Eventually I realized what it was. Just the year before, my beloved stepmother Virginia had died of cancer. She married my father when I was only five, so she'd been in my world most of my life. I missed her very much. Only eight months before she passed away, my best friend Mary had died unexpectedly. I missed her terribly every day.

Of all the people in my life who had passed on, these were the two who came to mind on St. Patrick's Day. Why? Because both Virginia and Mary were Irish American and proud of it. Mary had spent time in Ireland. Virginia had seldom even left the state, but she would have liked to have gone to Ireland. Once I realized what was nagging at me this morning—that I missed my two Irish loved ones on this St. Patrick's

Day—I allowed myself some time to think about them for a while. Then I got up and got to work.

A couple hours later, I was on a conference phone call that required simultaneous work on my computer screen. Out of the corner of my eye, I saw the herd of deer come into the yard and move slowly by the deck and slider. I glanced at them, but I didn't have opportunity to watch them. I was multi-tasking enough right then, and I knew they'd be back.

After the call, I poured another cup of coffee and returned to my computer chair. I glanced outside and saw that it had turned into a gorgeous morning—sunny and cloudless with a brilliant blue sky. Then I noticed something sitting in the yard just beyond the deck steps— something white and gleaming in the sun. Was it an animal?

I stood and looked out the slider door. No, it was not an animal. It was half of a buck's rack of antlers.

Even though I'm a country girl, I guess I always thought a buck's antler rack was one big thing—I didn't realize it is actually two separate halves. Here was a clean half sitting in the grass right next to my deck's steps.

I hurried outside and bent over the antlers. In all my years of country walks, I never came upon this. Had I looked up from my work, I would have seen the buck pushing it off his head only twenty feet away from me. And how I wish I had!

I picked up the antlers. It looked like this came from the same buck who'd been wandering through lately, because it was a small four-point rack. It shone bright white and was surprisingly heavy.

I took the rack indoors and set it on a table and studied it. It looked like a piece of sculpture, it was so perfectly made, with pretty serrations toward the base where it had cleanly broken off. My cat hopped up and began sniffing the object all over, especially that spot where it had once been physically attached to another creature.

Then I began to worry. Had I done the wrong thing by bringing this object indoors? There was talk of wasting disease with some deer in captivity in northern Michigan. Did I just expose my cat and myself to something dangerous?

I grabbed the phone and called my brother-in-law, Dick, a rancher and outdoorsman, someone to whom I take many of my nature questions. I caught him on his cell phone and told him what was up. He was even more excited than I was. "Do you know how lucky you are?" he said. "It's called a shed, and it's rare to find one like you just did. And usually the squirrels get to them right away, because they eat them for the calcium."

"Should I worry that I brought it into the house?"

"No, there's nothing dangerous in it," Dick said. "No seeds or anything. It's solid bone. Don't worry. Just consider yourself special."

So I did. I placed my lovely shed in a spot where I see it often. I'm not Irish, but on the day of the Irish saint, as I missed my Irish friend and my stepmom, I received right at my doorsteps what I decided to consider a personal gift—the shedding of a buck.

I had my own shedding that day. Some of my sadness went away because of that gorgeous gift. Now this piece of nature is a constant reminder to me that my loved ones are safe with God. And that God always has His eye on me.

# The Journey

## Crystal Ward Kent

*W*hen you bring a pet into your life, you begin a journey—a journey that will bring you more love and devotion than you have ever known, yet also test your strength and courage.

If you allow, the journey will teach you many things, about life, about yourself, and most of all, about love. You will come away changed forever, for one soul cannot touch another without leaving its mark.

Along the way, you will learn much about savoring life's simple pleasures—jumping in leaves, snoozing in the sun, the joy of puddles, and even the satisfaction of a good scratch behind the ears.

If you spend much time outside, you will be taught how to truly experience every element, for no rock, leaf or log will go unexamined, no rustling bush will be overlooked, and even the very air will be inhaled, pondered and noted as being full of valuable information. Your pace may be slower—except when heading home to the food dish—but you will become a better naturalist, having been taught by an expert in the field.

Too many times we hike on automatic pilot, our goal being to complete the trail rather than enjoy the journey. We miss the details—the colorful mushrooms on the rotting log, the honeycomb in the old maple snag, the hawk feather caught on a twig. Once we walk as a dog does, we discover a whole new world. We stop; we browse the landscape; we kick over leaves, peek in tree holes, look up, down, all around. And we learn what any dog knows: that nature has created a marvelously complex world that is full of surprises, that each cycle of the seasons brings ever-changing wonder, each day an essence all its own.

Even from indoors your will find yourself more attuned to the world around you. You will find yourself watching summer insects collecting on a screen (How bizarre they are! How many kinds there are!), or noting the flick and flash of fireflies through the dark. You will stop to observe the swirling dance of windblown leaves, or sniff the air after a rain. It does not matter that there is no objective in this; the point is in the doing, in not letting life's most important details slip by.

You will find yourself doing silly things that your pet-less friends might not understand: spending thirty minutes in the grocery aisle looking for the cat food brand your feline *must* have, buying dog birthday treats, or driving around the block an extra time because your pet enjoys the ride. You will roll in the snow, wrestle with chewy toys, bounce little rubber balls till your eyes cross, and even run around the house trailing your bathrobe tie—with a cat in hot pursuit—all in the name of love.

Your house will become muddier and hairier. You will wear less dark clothing and buy more lint rollers. You may find dog biscuits in your pocket or purse, and feel the need to explain that an old plastic shopping bag adorns your living room rug because your cat loves the crinkly sound.

You will learn the true measure of love—the steadfast, undying kind that says, "It doesn't matter where we are or what we do, or how life treats us as long as we are together." Respect this always. It is the most precious gift any living soul can give another. You will not find it often among the human race.

And you will learn humility. The look in my dog's eyes often made me feel ashamed. Such joy and love at my presence. She saw not some flawed human who would be cross and stubborn, moody or rude, but only her wonderful companion. Or maybe she saw those things and dismissed them as mere human foibles, not worth considering, and so chose to love me anyway.

If you pay attention and learn well, when the journey is done, you will be not just a better person, but the person your pet always knew you to be—the one they were proud to call beloved friend.

I must caution you that this journey is not without pain. Like all paths of true love, the pain is part of loving. For as surely as the sun sets, one day your dear animal companions will follow a trail you cannot yet go down. And you will have to find the strength and love to let them go. A pet's time on earth is far too short—especially for those who love them. We borrow them, really, just for a while, and during these brief years they are generous enough to give us all their love, every inch of their spirit and heart, until one day there is nothing left.

The cat that only yesterday was a kitten is all too soon old and frail and sleeping in the sun. The young pup with boundless energy wakes up stiff and lame, the muzzle now gray. Deep down we knew that this journey would end. We knew that if we gave our hearts they would be broken. But give them we must for it is all they ask in return. When the time comes, and the road curves ahead to a place we cannot see, we give one final gift and let them run on ahead—young and whole once more. "Godspeed, good friend," we say, until our journey comes full circle and our paths cross again.

# The Secret Life of Birds

*Adam Hunter*

*I* turned up the volume on my iPod and walked up the subway steps into the crisp New York City morning. Through a canyon of apartment buildings, I could just make out the trees of Central Park. I usually hit the park to play softball, but today I was there for something new: to join a group of birdwatchers to find some inspiration. Jeff, my contact, said to meet him at 7:00 AM. I wasn't thrilled. How inspiring can pigeons be this early in the morning?

I moved to the city eight years ago and loved the feeling of being in the center of it all. Sometimes, though, I missed the quiet of southern New Jersey. A few green city blocks couldn't compare to the fields and forests of the town where I grew up. Nearly every fall my family would feed two geese that took up residence on our lawn. There was something refreshing about being surrounded by the beauty of God's good earth, a sense of being connected to something greater. That was one thing Manhattan didn't have. Everything here was climate-controlled and built into a nice neat grid.

Jeff greeted me with binoculars. With him was Chuck, who'd intro-duced him to birding; Joe, a bird expert at the American Museum of Natural History; and Doug, his camera at the ready. "Is this your first time?" Jeff asked.

"I had a bird feeder once," I replied.

He smiled. "Hope we see something good!" We walked into the park. Suddenly, a flock of pigeons behind us rocketed into the air. "Look!" Jeff shouted. I turned and focused my binoculars. Just a bunch of pigeons, I thought. Or was it? The other guys were eagerly scanning the sky. "Do you see it?" Joe asked.

"I'm looking," Chuck said.

"What are we looking for?" I asked.

"A hawk," Joe said. A hawk! I'd heard about Pale Male and Lola, two red-tailed hawks that took up residence at the top of a high-rise, but I'd never seen one. I searched the sky, looking for the bird that had terrified the pigeons. A white feather floated in the breeze just as Jeff whispered, "There he is." Only a few feet away was the hawk. He stood at attention, surveying the area, his bright white, brown-speckled chest puffed out, so close I didn't need the binoculars to see what was clutched in his talons: a pigeon. My heart raced. This isn't supposed to happen here. This is the city, not the wild. The hawk stared at us, as if challenging us to approach. We didn't dare.

We headed toward The Ramble, a man-made thirty-eight-acre wilderness of trees on the north shore of Central Park Lake—a favorite spot for birders. "There are more than two hundred different species that have been spotted in the park," Jeff said. He started "listing" twenty-three years ago—writing down birds he spotted. Joe had seen 360 different birds in the city alone. A high-pitched warble stopped us. Once again we turned our binoculars toward the trees. "Yuck, a starling," Jeff said. The bird was perched on a high branch, its dark plumage shining. "Looks pretty to me," I said. It was "yuck" for a different reason, Joe said. In the 1880s, Eugene Schieffelin, a wealthy theater fanatic, brought European starlings to New York in an attempt to bring every bird mentioned in the works of Shakespeare to the United States. The starling was the only bird that thrived. Now some 140 million starlings live in North America, pushing out native songbirds from nesting areas.

The birds weren't even out in full force this time of year, but The Ramble seemed to explode with them. "Look," Jeff said, pointing out two Cooper's hawks. A yellow-bellied sapsucker clung to a treetop, scooping up bugs stuck in the sap. Two white-breasted nuthatches paced, waiting for a blue jay to vacate a feeder. A red-bellied woodpecker swooped in. A northern cardinal stood out in sharp contrast against a gray tree, singing a tune that seemed to hush the buzz of the city. Why didn't I notice the birds singing before?

We headed toward a spot where a long-eared owl had been holing up. "How do you know it's there?" I asked. Jeff explained that birders are a tight bunch—when a new bird is spotted in the city, a flurry of e-mails and phone calls alert everyone. Earlier that week they'd been excited by a Scott's oriole, usually found much farther south, in Union Square. "Union Square?" I said. That was by my apartment—a tiny bunch of trees surrounded by a hotel, a hospital and megastores. "That's another thing that keeps me coming out here," Jeff said. "The chance of seeing something unexpected."

The owl was nestled between the branches of a pine tree, a brown spot I would've missed had I not zeroed in with my binoculars. "What are you looking at?" a woman passing by asked.

"A long-eared owl," I said.

"Can I see?" I handed her my binoculars. A smile came across her face. I knew how she felt. Seeing something wild and free, here of all places, gave me the sense we weren't so cut off from nature. If an owl could find serenity here, maybe I could too.

Our last stop was beside the reservoir. By now I knew better than to dismiss the birds on the water as mere ducks. There were northern shovelers, buffleheads, hooded mergansers. All, Joe told me, were just visiting from distant locales. He'd been part of a research project on the migration patterns of terns. "I handled a bird in Argentina and discovered it was the same one I'd tagged in New York," he said.

Those geese in my front yard—was it possible they'd stopped first in New York and from my home flown to South America? Suddenly the city didn't seem so isolated. It was connected to nature by the flight patterns of thousands of birds, who found relief in the tiny green spaces I had overlooked. They were driven by a force more powerful than anything man could build, something truly Divine. "Come join us again," Jeff said, as I said my good-byes.

"I will," I told him. I meant it. Walking back to the subway, I kept my iPod turned off. I ignored the city traffic. Instead, I lifted my eyes to the trees and tuned my ears to listen to the sweet, lilting songs of the birds.

# It Happened in Bordentown

*Marilyn Carrier*

$\mathcal{S}$mall-town life never seems to change. I barely had to think about my daily routine as I went through it one morning in early spring. Grab a cup of coffee; make breakfast; kiss my husband, Tony, good-bye as he left for work; clear the table; and do the dishes. Next was my list of errands to get done around town.

I got in the car and drove past the old Roebling's factory, left behind from the days when Bordentown provided the steel cables for the Brooklyn and Golden Gate bridges, transporting them on the nearby Delaware River. The factory was long-closed now. *I doubt anything exciting has happened around here since*, I thought as I pulled up to my regular dry cleaner.

The man at the counter barely looked at me as I handed him my ticket. It was just the same at the supermarket. The cashier wearily rang me up. The woman behind me gave my groceries an impatient shove up the conveyer belt and started unloading her own purchases without a glance at me.

Clothes picked up and shopping done, I stopped in at the bakery to get something for dessert. The usual pastries. The counter was full of the familiar display of buns and cakes. I barely had to look at them to see the selection. My eyes were much more drawn to the woman ahead of me in line.

"Jumped clear out of the water!" she said as I stepped up behind her to pay. "Can you believe it? Right there in the Delaware River!"

The woman was bursting with excitement, waving her hands in the air as she talked. She looked so different from everyone else I'd seen that day. It was as if we were all in a black-and-white movie and she in brilliant Technicolor. What could possibly have happened around here to make her look like that?

"What was in the river?" I couldn't stop myself from asking.

The woman turned to me with a wide grin. "A whale!"

"A what?" I looked to the baker for a confirmation—maybe this woman was seeing things.

He shook his head and laughed. "She says there's a whale in the Delaware River. A big white whale. Craziest thing I've ever heard, but she swears it's true." He winked at me.

"You'll see," the woman promised us as she gathered up her bags. "Everyone will be talking about it."

I bought my own pastries and drove home to do the laundry. By the time I'd finished I'd forgotten the woman at the bakery with the wild story. After dinner Tony watched TV while I cleared up the dishes. "Marilyn," he called suddenly, "come quick! You've got to see this. You'll never believe it."

I ran into the room. He pointed at the television. A reporter was standing out by the river, the wind whipping through his hair. Tony turned up the sound.

"Local residents thought they must be dreaming when they saw a whale in the Delaware River, but this is no joke. The beluga white swam all the way from the Arctic to visit our area."

"Well, I'll be," I said. The woman at the bakery was right—there was a whale in the Delaware River. A whale named Helis, according to the news report. No wonder she had looked so excited. Imagine seeing a real live whale!

The next day when I went to the bank, everyone in line was buzzing. "I heard that Helis came here from Greenland," a man said.

"Or Russia," said a woman with a toddler around her leg. "My mother-in-law actually saw him break the surface. He blew a spray through his blowhole!"

"I want to see the whale! I want to see the whale!" her little boy shouted.

His mother squeezed his hand tight. "And I want to see the whale too, honey!"

"So do I!" I announced. Well, why not? It wasn't every day a whale came to Bordentown, New Jersey.

The next day was Saturday. Usually Tony and I spent the day doing things around the house. "How would you feel about going for a drive this afternoon?" I asked as we finished breakfast. "Maybe go down to the river?"

A smile broke out on Tony's face. "You mean go whale watching?" he said. "It's a date."

The shore was crowded with people by the time we got there. Several film crews were set up with bright lights. A lot of people had cameras. One family with children was crowded by a telescope. The children bounced around while their dad set everything up.

The fresh air blew in off the water, ruffling my hair. I took in a long, deep breath. We should get out here more often, I thought.

"See anything yet?" a woman with binoculars asked me.

We shook our heads.

"Me neither," she said. "But I'm sure he'll be up sometime."

"We saw him," two older women said proudly. In five minutes there was a whole circle of people swapping "fish" stories: people who saw the whale, people who knew people who saw the whale, people who thought they saw the whale, people who were convinced they'd see the whale if they were patient and kept looking. Tony and I joined right in.

We never saw Helis that day, but it still felt like a holiday. Tony and I started driving out to the river more often. Whenever there was a new Helis sighting we'd go directly to the spot. As the weeks went by, the weather got warmer and the trees began to blossom. I'd lived here for years. How had I never realized how beautiful Bordentown was in the spring?

More and more I appreciated the small-town world around me. It became part of my daily routine to smell the fresh air, gaze at the trees, feel the sun on my face. I wasn't the only one. Store owners took breaks to walk outside and stretch. The baker sold whale cookies in Helis's honor. Our minor-league baseball team, the Trenton Thunder, stopped playing when Helis appeared near the field. They ran over to get a look—and the opposing team ran right along with them, much to the coaches' frustration but to the crowd's delight!

Driving home along the interstate one evening in late spring, I marveled at how different life seemed since Helis came to town. How could a beluga whale have such an effect on people? I glanced at the river, orange and gold in the sunset. Something erupted through the surface. Helis's huge white head sparkled in the sun. He spouted a great fountain from his blowhole into the air. I held my breath as he rolled in the water. His fins were so graceful. They're like wings, I thought. Angel wings.

I knew my face was shining, just like that woman in the bakery. I had seen something special. Right here in Bordentown, New Jersey, where every day seemed special now, whale or no whale. What might tomorrow bring?

# Lessons from the Pack
## Jim Dutcher

One crisp autumn afternoon I hiked alone through a Rocky Mountain meadow, wondering if a dream I'd long cherished was dying. I'm a wildlife filmmaker, and I was camping out in the Sawtooth Mountains of Idaho to shoot a documentary about wolves. The film was to be an up-close, compelling portrait of a majestic but often misunderstood animal. Wolves, alternately feared as bloodthirsty predators and praised as symbols of the American wilderness, are wary and elusive creatures, extremely difficult to see in the wild, let alone film.

To capture them on camera in a relaxed state, I had formed a small wolf pack—two adults from wolf rescue centers and four pups born to other captive wolves—and designed a twenty-five-acre enclosure on the edge of a wilderness area where they could roam in a spacious natural habitat. My crew and I lived in a tent camp within the wolves' territory. We gave Native American names to the wolves to identify each one but made no attempt to teach the wolves their names or to initiate behavior or interaction. Our goal was to be a constant but unobtrusive presence, documenting daily life inside what we came to call the Sawtooth Pack.

That afternoon, though, as I hiked through the wolves' territory of alpine meadows, streams and forest, all I could think was how much had gone wrong in the year and a half since I'd begun. Though the project was miles from the nearest paved road, it was still in a part of the country where wolves' presence is controversial. From the beginning we had received anonymous letters warning, "Move the wolves immediately or we will!" The US Forest Service, which had issued permits allowing us on federal lands, was caught in the middle. I worried we would be forced to shut down.

Worse, the pack had failed to come together as I had hoped. Makuyi, the adult female, had developed cataracts and never bonded with the other wolves. Though we restored her vision with surgery, the ordeal broke her trust and we were forced to return her to the rescue center from which she had come. Akai, the adult male, had never taken to his role as pack leader and instead had become aggressive and dangerous. He too was sent back to a rescue center. Then, just that summer, one of my favorite wolves, Mo-taki, a young female, had been killed by a wild cougar. Her death brought a sadness to the pack, the crew and myself. Hiking through the wolves' territory, I sought solace from these setbacks in the autumn beauty of the mountains. Around me, aspen leaves twirled bright yellow. Far above, an eagle soared. I was hoping I'd come across the pack and be able to observe them for a while. I had no intention of filming or photographing them that day. I just wanted to be with the wolves and think about where the project was going.

As usual they were hard to spot. Their coats, thickening in anticipation of winter, provided near-perfect cover in the willows and meadow grasses. That didn't mean they weren't nearby. Often they'd materialize seemingly out of nowhere. Or I'd hike to one of the handful of places they liked to hang out. Wolves are naturally territorial, and the Sawtooth Pack was no exception. Even with twenty-five acres to roam, they'd picked a few spots—the meadow, some groves of aspen, the edge of an old beaver pond—where I was almost always sure to find them. I walked on, contemplating my troubles.

Suddenly a long, lean wolf glided out from a patch of trees and loped toward me. I stopped. It was Kamots, one of the pups we had introduced. Actually, now a year and a half old, Kamots was no longer a pup. He was an impressive young male wolf, with a splendid dark gray coat shading to white on his belly and legs. I crouched and watched him approach. Almost from the day he was born, Kamots had shown himself to be the most alert, curious and self-assured of the Sawtooth wolves. Though I had always assumed that Akai would lead the pack as its alpha male, it was Kamots who day by day ascended the hierarchy with barely a whimper from the older wolf. There wasn't a more scientific way to describe his demeanor. He simply behaved with confidence.

As he often did, Kamots came right up to greet me. This time, however, instead of trotting back off to wherever he had been, he sat down on his haunches and looked at me quizzically. Wolves are large creatures, and Kamots' calm expression filled my vision. For a moment I sat there regarding him. Though I had done considerable research on the social hierarchy of wolf packs, it was only after watching Kamots that I learned how a natural-born alpha behaves. Kamots held his tail and head high. He was continually vigilant, not simply responding to obvious threats but maintaining a watchful eye at all times. When a strange sound rang out in the forest, Kamots was the first to trot off to investigate. Perhaps the rest of the pack did not behave this way because they knew they didn't need to. They knew Kamots would keep them safe.

I looked at Kamots now and suddenly knew who the strong leader my project so desperately needed was. It was Kamots. He had the power and the wisdom to guide the pack into a new stability. I could feel an understanding between us, a cooperation that had not occurred with Akai.

Just then, in a gesture I had never seen before, Kamots raised his paw and stretched his foreleg toward me. I held my hand out to meet it and we sat there, palm to paw. At that moment his strength and stillness were more reassuring than any words from another human being could be. It occurred to me—if I could just hold up my end, Kamots would hold up his. I was still absorbing this when Kamots took his paw away and trotted back into the forest. I was alone again. And a great peace settled over me, a peace I hadn't felt in my life in a very long time.

Over the course of the next year, the project's fortunes improved. Jamie, a woman I had met several years before, joined the crew. She'd worked in the animal hospital at the National Zoo in Washington, DC, and shared my love for wildlife. She brought with her a knowledge of animal husbandry and medical care. Combined with her gentle instinct, these skills enabled her to quickly gain access to the sensitive and se-cret inner lives of the wolves. At the same time, the wolves matured and established a cohesive hierarchy under Kamots. He and the pack's alpha female, Chemukh, mated and produced offspring. These pups were pos-sibly the first wolves born in the Sawtooth Mountains in more than half a century.

A few days after the pups' arrival, Chemukh allowed Jamie to inspect her litter. Ordinarily wolves are fiercely protective of their young, and it would be foolhardy for any human to approach a wolf's den. Jamie, how-ever, had earned the Sawtooth Pack's trust. As I watched in amazement, she disappeared into Chemukh's den with a flashlight. Five feet inside, she found herself face to face with four tiny balls of fur, eyes still closed, noses raised to catch a human's strange scent. When Jamie reappeared, Chemukh was sitting patiently by the entrance, her head cocked in cu-riosity. Then she gave Jamie's face a lick and re-entered her den. It was a miraculous moment.

Even as the project continued, Jamie and I looked forward to future work documenting other creatures and ecosystems in North

America and beyond. But something changed. The original two-year project grew to four years, then six. One film became two, then three. What began as a fascination with wolves became a passion and, finally, a life calling that has only grown stronger with the passing years. It has drawn us far from our familiar role of filmmakers into the center of fierce controversy currently raging over wolf management. Today, Jamie and I are married, and full-time advocates for wolves, traveling the country sharing what we learned during our six years in the Sawtooths.

Speaking to schools, museums and community groups, we recall our face-to-face encounters with Kamots and his pack. We explain that wolves are not just predators, but also family animals who play and hunt as a team, care for their injured, take turns looking after pups and mourn their dead. Without these misunderstood animals, America's wild places risk becoming perilously unbalanced. In Yellowstone National Park alone, the reintroduction of a mere thirty-one wolves in the mid-1990s healed decades of damage to the park's ecosystem that had built up after wolves were exterminated in the 1920s. In just a few years the wolves dramatically strengthened elk herds by culling out weak and sick animals. Willows and aspens, long decimated by overpopulated elk, regrew along stream banks. Trout returned to shady, cooler streams. Beavers built dams. Migratory birds flocked to new wetlands. An entire park was revitalized by thirty-one wolves.

Our hope is that people are beginning to know wolves as caring animals devoted to their families, animals that deserve a chance to survive. We believe the wolves of the Sawtooth Pack were trailblazers for their wilder cousins, opening peoples' eyes, serving as ambassadors from their kind to ours.

A wild wolf seldom lives beyond seven years—a captive wolf can sometimes live a few years longer. Most of the Sawtooth Pack now exists only in memory. What we will never forget, however, is the gift Kamots and his pack gave us—their trust. It is why Jamie and I consider the time we spent with them as the richest, most rewarding, most beautiful experience of our lives. And it is why I will always remember the wolf who reached out that crisp autumn afternoon and guided his pack and me through troubled times.

# Country Surprise

*Lynn Seely*

*I* reside in the northeast corner of Pennsylvania. In October, few places can compare to the splendor of the fall foliage.

Local farmers grow a variety of crops here, and their neat well-kept farms are scattered throughout the rolling countryside. Apples are particularly sweet this time of year due to the cooler weather. Pumpkins are in abundance. It is quite a pretty sight to see the bright, vividly orange pumpkins nestled in the straw-colored grass of farmers' fields.

I enjoy taking a daily walk and this morning was particularly lovely. What a treat to have such a clear blue sky, and the fall colors were beautiful too. After thirty minutes I arrived at one of my favorite areas near a field and decided to rest for a bit. The trees surrounding part of the field wore brilliant russet leaves, as well as yellow, orange and gold. The partially forested mountain in the background, just behind the field, displayed those colors too, in addition to deep green from the pine trees that grew on the rocky, windswept granite cliffs.

After a short rest, it was time for me to head back home. Suddenly a movement caught my eye.

A pumpkin had just rolled uphill. *Uphill?*

Wait a minute! That wasn't possible. But I *had* seen it happen! Or had I?

Intrigued, I decided to go closer and get a better look. As I stepped off the road and into the field, I startled a pair of quail from their hiding place in the dry grass. Of the three of us, it was I who was the most startled!

My attention was soon focused on the pumpkin patch again. Had I been seeing things, I wondered? Everything was very still. Everything was as it should be, beautiful and quiet. I shrugged. I decided it must have been an illusion, or my active imagination at work. But just as I decided to leave, I saw the pumpkin move again!

To my utter amazement, I watched as the pumpkin wobbled slowly *uphill!*

Very strange! Very strange indeed!

I walked slowly, trying my best to be very quiet. I didn't want that pumpkin aware that I was approaching it. I knew that there had to be some logical reason for a pumpkin to be rolling uphill, but at the moment I couldn't think of one! I crept closer to the rolling pumpkin. Now I was within five feet of it. The pumpkin suddenly stopped moving and I froze in place.

I waited.

It seemed to be waiting too.

I finally decided I had to know for certain how a pumpkin traveled uphill, all by itself in the middle of a field. I walked up to the pumpkin and nudged it with my foot. It moved easily; nothing unusual here. I nudged it again.

Suddenly, I saw two small creatures streak away from the pumpkin. Startled, I jumped back as I watched them flee. They finally paused at a large boulder about fifty feet from me and scrambled up on top of it. Two sets of small brown eyes glared at me. Their scolding barks reproved me, as they boisterously expressed their displeasure at my intrusion into their life!

Well, good gracious, it was a pair of chipmunks!

While their warning barks filled the air, I knelt down and took a closer look at the pumpkin. Several large holes were visible on the end nearest me. I looked inside and saw to my surprise that the pumpkin was almost hollow.

I assumed that they must have been eating and by chance the pumpkin was rolled about by them as they ate.

But no, I soon found out that wasn't the case.

As I left the field I continued watching them. The chipmunks finally lost interest in me once I got farther away. They began racing around the field at great speed and they also jumped from one pumpkin to another. Finally, they raced toward the hollowed out pumpkin and leapt inside. It began to roll this way and that. It was clear they were playing.

Every year since then, once Halloween is over, I take my carved pumpkins to the edge of that field for them to play in. For a few weeks after that when I pass by on my daily walk I often see the chipmunks playing. Sometimes they are racing about the field—sometimes sitting on the boulder in the morning sun—and sometimes I see one or two striped faces peering back at me from the crooked grin of a pumpkin.

# Martita's Door

### Lisa Diaz

*R*ows of mourners filled the ancient wooden pews of the centuries-old church, so different from the modern churches I was used to in America. Everything about Antigua, Guatemala, was different and beautiful to me: majestic cathedrals, cobblestone streets and distant volcanoes. I only wished I were visiting for a happier reason. My husband, Oscar, and I had flown back to his home to attend his mother's funeral, my first visit. I mourned for Oscar's loss and for myself as well. How I wished I had been able to get to know Martita Diaz, my mother-in-law.

I struggled to follow the priest's eulogy in Spanish. I could well imagine what he might be saying. I had heard so many stories about Martita since I'd met Oscar, how she seemed to be like a mother to everyone she met.

Oscar told me he often came home from school and found her chatting with a stranger. When he asked who the person was, his mother said, "Just someone who needed someone to talk to." He described her cooking in her tiny kitchen, boiling giant pots on the stove—pots she could hardly lift on her own. She wasn't cooking just for her family, but for anyone who might be hungry and had no money for food themselves. Word got around about the kind lady who fed the poor, and Martita's church listed her house as an official soup kitchen.

If Martita made such an impression on me, I thought, looking around at the others gathered in her memory, what must she have meant to the people she saw every day here in Antigua?

I heard footsteps in the center aisle and turned to look. A scruffy golden-brown dog trotted into the church. How did that dog get in here? I love animals, but the church was God's house and a dog did not belong in it. Someone would have to shoo the animal out.

Without fanfare, the dog walked right up to the altar and sat down as if she were a noble guard. No one made a move. I turned my attention back to the priest, but found it hard to concentrate. My eyes kept wandering back to that silly animal, sitting so proudly by the coffin. As if she had some purpose here. *Don't be ridiculous*, I thought. *She's just wandered in where she doesn't belong.*

I hoped no one else was distracted. Such a shame for something like this to happen during Martita's funeral. For all my mother-in-law had done for others, she deserved a respectful service. Now this annoying dog had ruined it.

At the end of the service, we all rose to follow Martita's coffin in a procession to the cemetery at the bottom of the hill. The dog got up too and led the way down the aisle.

"Why doesn't someone tie that animal up?" I whispered to Oscar.

"She's not bothering anyone," Oscar said with a shrug.

We walked out to the cobblestone road that led to the cemetery. I got into a car with my husband behind the hearse. The other mourners followed on foot. As we drove slowly down the road I looked out the back window. The golden-haired dog trotted right behind us. The other mourners were supposed to be following our car, but it looked more like they were following the golden dog right through the big iron gates.

At the burial site we gathered around the mausoleum and watched as the coffin was placed inside. Oscar read a tribute he had written for his mother. "*Las puertas de mi madre*," he said, "*siempre estaban abiertas para quienes necesitaban ayuda.*" My mother's door was always open to those in need.

The dog sat in front, listening, it seemed, to every word Oscar said.

When Oscar finished, the mourners filed back out of the cemetery. The golden dog sat by the mausoleum until they had all gone. Then she turned and with slow, deliberate steps, walked out of the cemetery's iron gates.

Only the family and the priest were left behind. His eyes followed the dog walking beyond the gates. "The dog has never come into the church before," he said.

"So why would she come to a funeral?" I wondered.

"She is a street dog," the priest explained. "She has no home, no one to belong to. But there was one place she was always welcome. Martita fed her every day, just as she fed the others who needed her help."

I looked back at the golden dog, now making her way up the cobblestone street. I had thought she had no place at a church service. But everyone—strays of any kind—had a place in God's house. He turned away no one. Martita had lived her life following God's example. What better place than at her funeral for me to learn to follow hers?

# One Incredible Journey

*Amy Collins*

$\mathcal{W}$e worry about the weather out here in Oklahoma, maybe more than most folks, especially in spring when vicious storms and tornadoes can gather deadly strength in the course of an afternoon. One minute the sun is shining and the next you're running to the basement for shelter. But that spring seven years ago, there was little that could dampen my happiness. Just months earlier I'd given birth to twin girls, Emerson and Preslee. Harley, our Dalmatian, had a litter of twelve pups. One was very special.

We called her "Muff" because her brown ears made it look as if she were wearing tiny earmuffs. Dalmatian puppies are usually all white—the spots come later—but Muff stood out with her solid brown ears. We gave away the other puppies, but kept Muff for ourselves. The perfect puppy for my babies, I thought. "They'll all grow up together," I told my mom.

One blustery afternoon early that May, Muff and Harley didn't come back from playing outside. "Muff!" I shouted into the whipping wind. "Harley! Where are you?" May is the heart of tornado season out here, and there were reports of dangerous storms coming. I was worried. "They'll come back. They probably chased a rabbit or something," my husband, Brian, tried to assure me. "Dogs can always find their way back home."

But the next day they still weren't back, and the weather was worse, much worse. I called the animal shelter, drove around town, checked with the neighbors. I was at my mom's place when she said, "There's a tornado coming and it looks real bad." I scanned the darkening horizon, the sky bruised with storm clouds. "Lord," I said, "keep my dogs safe, especially Muff. She's just a pup."

We took shelter in a nearby elementary school basement. Even down there I could hear the wind howling mercilessly outside. Still, I couldn't stop thinking about Harley and Muff. Were they stuck out in the storm? I almost hoped they had been stolen. Then at least they'd be out of harm's way. Harley was older and could take care of herself, but Muff would be helpless. All at once the wind's howl turned to an incredible roar, like we were being run over by a freight train, and even my worries about the dogs were drowned out by it.

Finally it was over. The first thing I did was search for Muff and Harley. Driving around town, I realized how lucky my family had been. The tornado left a swath of unbelievable destruction less than a half mile from our house. The humane society shelter was chaotic—bursting at the seams with dogs and cats gone stray in the storm. Their eyes all searched desperately for a familiar face to claim them. But no Harley. No Muff.

Six months after the tornado, we moved into a new house fifteen miles away. I still worried about the dogs. What if they came back to the old home and didn't find us there? Where would they go then? I knew I was being unrealistic, but I still held out hope. It was a hope that faded with time, especially for Harley, but once you have a dog you never forget him. I always wondered about poor little Muff with those cute brown ears. The years passed, and we got two new dogs—a Dachshund and a Labrador retriever. The girls grew up playing with them. But my heart still skipped a beat anytime I saw a Dalmatian.

Then, six years after that terrible tornado season, on a Saturday afternoon a week before Easter, my mom called. She told me she and my sister had been surfing the Internet when they came across the Web site of Rocky Spot Rescue, a local organization that puts dogs up for adoption. "We don't need another dog," I started to say, but she cut me off. "I think you need to see this," she said.

I turned on my computer and clicked to the Web site. I scrolled down to the photograph of the dog Mom told me about. Chills ran down my spine. Those ears, just like earmuffs. The Web site said this dog—named Ginger—had originally been rescued a week after the tornado six years ago. Could it be Muff?

Brian was cautious. "Lots of dogs got picked up after the tornado. I bet a bunch were Dalmatians," he said. "Besides, do we have room for a third dog?"

"The shelter is hosting an open adoption at the pet store tomorrow," I told him. "I have to act on this. Otherwise, I'll always wonder if it was her."

"Okay," he said. "We'll all go tomorrow. But don't get your hopes up, hon."

Getting ready for bed that night, I had my doubts. What had become of Muff in six years? Why was she still up for adoption? Even if it were her, after six years, would she remember us? How could we even be sure it was her? She was only a puppy when she disappeared. I called my mom. "Maybe I should just let it be," I sighed. "Nonsense," Mom assured me. "A dog never forgets a scent. If this dog is Muff, she will know you."

Sunday afternoon—Palm Sunday—we all piled into our SUV and headed to the pet store. My hands clutched a bunch of Muff's puppy pictures. The girls talked excitedly about having a new dog to play with. "Now, don't get too excited," Brian said to them. "We're just going to check this out."

"But if it is Muff, we'll get her, right?" Emerson said.

My husband gave me a look. "We'll see," I said.

The second I entered the pet store, my eyes scanned the dogs lined up for adoption. There were many Dalmatians, but none had those ears. I went up to one of the shelter volunteers. "Excuse me, but do you still have the Dalmatian you called Ginger?"

"Yes," she said, "but she's not available for adoption now. She's recuperating from a dog bite."

"Can we see her?" I couldn't hide my excitement.

"Why her?" the volunteer inquired.

"Because . . ." I said hesitantly, "I think she's our dog."

I handed her Muff's puppy photos. She flipped through them, eyes wide with disbelief. "Those ears look familiar, all right," she agreed. "I'll call the shelter right away and tell them about you. I'll let them know you're coming down." She gave us directions and we drove off.

All the way to the shelter, my heart pounded. Please let it be Muff. Please let her remember us. As we pulled up, I could see a bunch of dogs in the fenced-in yard, some running around playing, others lazing in the shade. One Dalmatian stood at the fence. The car came to a stop and the dog turned toward us. I stepped out and called to her, "Muff?"

There was not even a moment of hesitation. The instant she heard my voice, she started to bark happily. She put her paws up on the fence, then tried to climb it, jumping up and down. The shelter employees came outside to see what all the commotion was about. "She doesn't react that way to anybody," one of them said to me. "She's usually so shy."

They let me in, and the dog almost bowled me over. I kneeled down and put my arms around her. She was all over me, licking my face, barking, nuzzling against my chest. She was a whole lot bigger now, and filled out, but there was no mistaking that this dog knew exactly who I was. I held her head and looked deep into her eyes. "It's her," I shouted out. "It's Muff!"

"Amy," Brian said, his voice choking with emotion, "this dog definitely has to come home with us."

It took us a while to find where our poor puppy had been the past six years. Rocky Spot had rescued her from the animal welfare division just days before she was scheduled to be euthanized. Her first adoptive parents after the tornado couldn't care for her after she was hit by a car and broke her hip. Her next owners moved and left her behind, tied to a tree. She had other traumas and travails that I couldn't even believe. But miraculously, she survived it all. And I don't use *miraculously* as a figure of speech.

We call her Ginger now, but she'll always be Muff to me. The kids got their new dog and I got my old one back. That first Easter Sunday, Muff—Ginger—and I went for a walk, just the two of us. She kept close, walking contentedly at my side, occasionally looking at me as if she couldn't believe it. I knew how she felt. I could still remember clear as ever that day of the tornado when I searched the neighborhood for her, shouting into the rising wind. But my prayers too had been taken up by that same wind to the only One who could keep my dog safe when I could not. Now at last, she'd come home.

# The Parrots of January

### Rosie Schaap

*T*he seventh of January and already the excitement of starting a new year had faded. All that seemed to remain of Christmas? A brittle, dried-up balsam tree in a corner of my living room. I took down the ornaments, unraveled the strings of lights and unhooked the star from the top. I pulled the cardboard storage boxes out of the closet and got to work.

Yes, the holiday season was over, and I had a serious case of winter-time blues.

Bundled in a thick coat and scarf, and a knitted wool hat with earflaps, I trudged down my stoop in heavy boots. The New York City Parks Department had been hosting a "Mulchfest" for ten years, and this year there was a site at historic Green-Wood Cemetery, just blocks away. I didn't really feel like going out, but I loved the idea of mulch from my tree nourishing plantings around the city. I suppose it's not every day you see someone pushing a red, wire-mesh shopping cart loaded up with an expired Christmas tree down Fifth Avenue, the "Main Street" of my Brooklyn neighborhood. My neighbor Mrs. Arroyo broke into a big grin when she saw me coming. Leaning in front of their corner grocery store, the Zawisny brothers did a double take. Despite the bitter cold—the temperature hovered just a few degrees above freezing—the sun shone brightly on the residents of Greenwood Heights. I just wished it could do a better job warming me up.

The high, ornate spires of the cemetery's Gothic gatehouse rose before me up a slight hill, like a vision from the cover of a Victorian novel. I followed the handwritten signs to the mulching station and looped my cart around the path. A small group of people had gathered in bulky parkas and mufflers, watching their trees go through the chipper. I couldn't bear to look. I dropped mine off, and turned toward home, but something stopped me in my tracks.

"*Grr-rak! Grrak!*" I heard. What was that? Definitely not a pigeon—nor was it a sparrow, nor a starling. It was utterly unlike the sound of any of the birds I knew from nearly a lifetime in the city. I looked up and could hardly believe my eyes: In the trees I spied more than a dozen diminutive, vivid-green parrots with pale-gray bellies and yellow beaks, perched on bare branches. I heard more squawking coming from the gatehouse spires. Way up in carved stone niches, tiny emerald heads poked out of nests.

"*Grr-rak! Grrak! Grr-rak!*"

Wild parrots! In the middle of Brooklyn? In January?

I'd heard stories about wild parrots in the city from time to time when I was growing up. I'd almost written them off as urban legends—like the albino crocodiles that are said to dwell in the sewers beneath Manhattan. But there the parrots were, in all their colorful glory. The birds flew swiftly and gracefully from the spires to the trees and back again, chattering exuberantly the whole time. All the folks who had come to have their trees mulched lifted their heads to the skies, including me.

"There's another one!" a little girl said to her dad, pointing up.

"Ah, yes," a knowledgeable Brooklynite explained, "I believe they are members of the species Myiopsitta Monachus—monk parrots."

They certainly weren't as quiet as monks, but still, the name seemed just right: There was something magical, something sacred even, about their unexpected presence in the midst of a hectic metropolis on a cold January day. Soon every last person in this group of strangers was riveted by the parrots' antics. They were natural entertainers. Each bird seemed to have its own distinctive personality. How could I possibly go home? Suddenly, it didn't even feel so cold outside anymore, though the temperature hadn't risen at all.

I lingered at Green-Wood for the better part of an hour, observing the parrots swoop and play and fuss over their elaborately crafted nests. Amid the skyscrapers and subways and hustle and bustle of the city, I often feel distant from nature, detached. Yet somehow I'd found nature—or it had found me—less than ten blocks from home. I thought of those three startling words from a poem by William Wordsworth, later used by C. S. Lewis as the title of his memoir: *Surprised by Joy*. That's exactly how I felt.

Joy. It can be difficult to sustain the joy held out by the holidays, the feelings of wonder and astonishment. I thought I'd let those feelings slip beyond my grasp. But the wild parrots of Brooklyn reminded me that all things are possible. Even in the city, nature is never far away, and always ready to surprise us with the powerful joy that it is uniquely and beautifully equipped to bestow.

# The Delightful Mrs. S

## Lynn Seely

*T*ap, tap, tap.

The light tapping sound gently roused me from slumber. I stayed under the covers and listened to the soft tapping. A small branch was intermittently rapping against the window as a morning breeze stirred.

*Tap, Tap, Tap!*

This time the rapping was louder, more insistent. Now fully awake, I realized it was not a branch making the sound; it was probably Mrs. S tapping on my window. My old alarm clock had failed me yet again. I knew I had better get up immediately or I'd be in for quite a scolding.

The first time I saw Mrs. S was on a cool spring morning. I looked out my bedroom window and saw a white squirrel sitting in the branches of my Sycamore. The tree grows close to my house and its smooth branches and green leaves create a shady canopy over a small porch roof below my window. The tree then stretches up another twenty feet or so above the roof of my two-story house. I felt as if I were in a tree house when I looked out my window. I loved it.

I have always been of the opinion that squirrels were cute and clever, so that first morning I decided to put some peanuts outside my window to see if the squirrel would eat them. She was very wary of me as I opened the window and dropped a handful of nuts outside, yet as soon as I closed the window she decided it was worth the risk to investigate. She cautiously made her way to the irresistible pile then quickly grabbed a treat and scampered away. Once back in the safety of the tree she leisurely ate the peanut. When she finished, she folded her little arms across her chest, waved her tail a few times and observed me for a few minutes.

When she was satisfied that I wasn't going to chase her, she decided to return to the pile of nuts. She realized that for some very odd reason I had thrown away perfectly good food. If I didn't want it, then she would be happy to dispose of it. The sheltered roof made a cozy balcony for my little visitor. She was concealed from view when she was there. She felt quite safe so high above the sidewalk and street.

In time, we got to know one another better. She would linger a little longer each morning. She soon lost her wariness of me and grew quite unafraid. As she ate her peanut she would observe me with bright-eyed interest. It would seem she was as interested in me, as I was in her. I began calling her Mrs. S, and when I would speak to her, she would acknowledge me with a gentle wave of her fluffy tail and a bold look right into my eyes.

Eventually Mrs. S began taking the peanuts right out of my hand. She wanted all those unwanted peanuts and although she could not fathom why I would discard perfectly good food, she was sure she should be the one to benefit from this strange practice of mine. The peanuts were particularly appreciated by Mrs. S during the cold winter.

Then one morning I heard a tap on my window. I could not imagine what was making the noise. I went toward the sound and peered out my window and saw Mrs. S staring in. She seemed extremely annoyed that I had forgotten to put out any nuts. There was no mistake that she was scolding me with her loud chatter. But that wasn't enough. Apparently Mrs. S thought I needed a reminder as to why she was at the window in the first place, so as I watched, she tucked one arm close to her chest and with the other rapped loudly on the window. This produced a peal of laughter from me and an immediate reward for her. I opened the window and gave Mrs. S an apology as well as an extra-large helping of peanuts. It was a lesson she never forgot. From that day on, she preferred to tap on the window in hopes of getting extra peanuts even if a pile of peanuts was right in front of her. She thought this was a wonderful way to get extra nuts. She was, of course, correct.

As the weeks passed I noticed Mrs. Squirrel was getting really plump. Then she disappeared for days and the peanuts lay untouched. I feared the worst.

Finally one morning, I heard the familiar tapping at the window. Mrs. S was back! She certainly was much leaner and seemed very hungry. I was relieved to see her and I told her so. She cocked her head this way and that as I talked to her while she munched away on her delicious peanuts.

Things soon got back to normal and she resumed her usual activities. She would *tap, tap, tap,* and I would happily oblige her with as many peanuts as she wanted.

A few weeks after the return, she brought me a big surprise. One morning I found myself looking at miniature versions of Mrs. S. There, waiting a short distance away, were two gray baby squirrels! She was a mother and had brought her babies with her this morning. They stayed farther away and watched carefully as their mother showed them all the tricks of getting food at this place. They seemed extremely puzzled that their mother would tap on the window. It must have seemed very un-squirrel like to them.

In time the babies became brave enough to eat the nuts while I was in view. Each morning I always had three little faces peering in the window as they waited to be fed. Mrs. S had done a fine job of raising her babies and teaching them all her skills.

As I made my way to the window this morning I thought Mrs. S would probably scold me as I had not put out any food yet.

*Tap, Tap, Tap! Tap, tap, tap!*

To my surprise, I saw it was the babies that had rapped on the window! Both babies glanced over their shoulders to see if their momma was watching them. Mrs. S waved her tail in approval before she moved closer. Peanuts in hand, I stood frozen, not wanting to startle them.

As I stood there, all three started rapping on the window at once.

*Tap, Tap, Tap!*

Breakfast was wanted, now!

I was laughing as I opened the window and placed the peanuts out. Each grabbed a peanut and skillfully used little fingers to remove the shell before eating the nut.

I thought about the supplies I was going to buy later that day. I definitely needed more peanuts but I decided there was one item that I would remove from my list—a new alarm clock. After all, waking up to a loud ringing was not nearly as pleasant as waking to a soft *tap, tap, tap*.

# Small Miracles

*Lonnie Hull Dupont*

*O*ne chilly March evening, my husband Joe and I were getting ready to settle in for the night when we heard a little cry outside. Although we live in a fairly remote area, we are on a state road that has a fair number of big trucks. To hear such a small cry was unusual.

It got louder and more insistent. I looked out the front door, and there, sitting in a pool of light from our window, sat the homeliest little half-kitten/half-cat. She was all mouth, looking me right in the eye, crying for something to eat. She was around six months old, scrawny and missing some teeth, and, boy, was she loud!

"What should we do?" my husband said.

"Well, we have to feed her out back," I said. "We can't let her go hungry." I thought for a moment and added, "And you have to do it. I'll get attached, and she's just going to get run over by a truck. You have to feed her."

My husband nodded. "I'm allergic to cats, so you know I won't get attached."

Famous last words. When Joe came in later, he was visibly moved. "She drooled right on the ground, she was so hungry," he reported. "But she rubbed and rubbed on me first, as if she were thanking me."

Joe fed her out by the barn for the next several weeks. My husband's allergies kept us from letting her in, but she seemed not to want to come inside anyway. She was skittish and seemed to like being outside as long as she was fed. She was clearly taking care of herself, not being hounded by the wild animals around here. Spring came early and warm that year, so life wasn't too bad for the cat.

What Joe hadn't told me was the he and the cat were bonding. He would tap a can against the barn and she'd sashay her way to him, then rub on him. He'd pick her up, place her forehead against his, and they would just be that way for a while. Then he'd put her by her food where she hunkered down and ate. All the time she ate, Joe would pet her back really hard. She loved it. I think it made her feel safe, and in a primitive way, she had another creature literally to watch her back while she ate in the wild.

But we knew our place was dangerous. Strays never seemed to survive the truck traffic. And though it was spring, we knew winter in Michigan is no place for outdoor cats. We had no shelter for her—the barn was not ours and was locked up. We couldn't let her in the house because of Joe's allergy—he always had allergy attacks at houses with pet cats.

My brother-in-law offered to take her for his barn. He had a longhorn steer ranch and could use a mouser. That wouldn't be a bad life for a cat who seemed to like the outdoors—she'd have plenty of warm hay to sleep in and daily human interaction. So one night we put the cat in a travel box and drove the eight miles to the ranch. She cried most of the way, and we talked soothingly to her. At the ranch, she was unnerved, but eventually she sat down and ate, then began grooming. We left.

But I was in tears. I felt we'd abandoned an animal that had clearly been abandoned once before. Joe reminded me that we were trying to help a scrappy little cat survive, that it really was a good thing. I felt sick to my stomach about leaving her, but I had to agree.

Ten nights later, Joe walked by the front door and glanced out. There in a pool of light sat the cat, looking him straight in the eye, this time quietly.

"You won't believe this," Joe said. "Look."

Sure enough, there she sat, skinny and dirty. She had unusual markings, so there was no doubt it was she. She had walked eight miles of swamps, cornfields, wild animals, dogs and gun-happy people who hate cats, and she'd crossed the dangerous road of trucks to get to us.

Joe and I looked at each other. In unison we said, "She stays." We opened the door, and the little stray walked in as if she'd always lived here.

"What about your allergy?" I asked.

"I'll take a decongestant," Joe said. "This cat walked back to us."

Used to the outdoors, the cat had some trouble with the first night indoors. But she was exhausted, and after wolfing down food, she fell sound asleep. We named her Kit Kat after the kitchen clock.

The next day, Joe dropped off Kit Kat at a vet's for shots and spaying, and the following day we went to pick her up. There was bad news.

"Your cat has a terminal illness," the vet said. "When we opened her up, we saw that she has feline infectious peritonitis in the advanced stage. Lots of strays and feral cats get this. She is asymptomatic right now, but she isn't going to live a long life."

We were devastated. After much questioning, it turned out that Kit Kat probably didn't even have a year. "We can put her down if you'd like," the vet offered.

Before I had a chance to respond, Joe said firmly, "Absolutely not. This cat is a survivor, and she worked hard to get back to us. We'll take her home and keep her until she dies."

And so we took home our dying cat. That night, with stitches in her belly and a fresh pedicure, she caught a mouse. We were as pleased as could be.

Something else was going in my life at the time. I was adopted at birth and had found the whereabouts of my biological mother many years ago. I wrote to her several times—even asked for a medical history—but she never answered my letters. I could not know at the time that the night we took Kit Kat to the ranch, my mother died in a nearby town. I had never met her. Three days later, her friends tracked me down. They hadn't known she had a child at all until shortly before she died, and then only because they came across my letters. The letters were kept together in a place near her reading chair. For some reason, she could never bring herself to respond to me.

The day after we brought Kit Kat home from the vet, I went to my mother's memorial service. I learned that she had a wonderful laugh, that her confirmation verse had been "Make a joyful noise unto the Lord." I learned that her favorite song was "Mack the Knife," a detail I personally found particularly delightful for some reason. And that, like me, she was a voracious reader. I got to know her friends and my relatives. I was so happy that I had at least this much. Probably only adopted people can really understand this, but at the age of forty-six, for the first time in my life I felt grounded.

But I couldn't grieve. I felt distanced. After all, I did not know this woman. She gave birth to me, but I never knew her. I felt oddly detached among the mourners. I only wished she would have consented to see me before dying.

Back home, however, I suddenly found all kinds of maternal feelings rising in me toward Kit Kat. I have no children and had never felt these feelings before. But I found myself rocking Kit Kat and crying. Why was I crying? On the surface, I didn't want my little cat to die. But I really knew that she was the vehicle to help me connect to my deeply buried grief about the woman who bore me but would not know me.

Kit Kat would tolerate this for a while, then she would jump down and go about her cat day. And I'd feel better. But I always prayed that I'd be able to handle it when she got sick.

Months went by. She didn't get sick. She got fat and sleek and turned into a gorgeous tortoiseshell. She was smart and quick, and she lived for Joe, who would get right down on the floor and play with her. She still liked us to watch her while she ate. Sometimes, if we left her alone for the day, she wouldn't eat until we came back and sat with her at her cat dish.

Joe took drugs for his allergies, and we agreed to keep Kit Kat out of the bedroom, thereby keeping one room dander-free. But Joe's allergy simply disappeared. Now both my cat and my husband were healthier than they were suppose to be!

After a few months, I took Kit Kat in to get her claws trimmed. It was the same clinic but a different vet. "How do you think her FIP is?" I asked.

The vet looked at me then back at Kit Kat. "This cat has FIP?" she asked. "Who told you that?"

I paused. "This clinic told me."

The vet looked a little uncomfortable. "Did they see it in wet stages when they operated on her?"

"Yes," I said. "Doesn't she have it?"

"Well," she drawled, "sometimes other things look like FIP. The fact that your cat not only did not get sick but in fact got healthier makes me wonder. I'm not saying she has it, but I'm not saying she doesn't, either."

There is no test for FIP, so I took Kit Kat home, hardly daring to believe she might not die so soon.

Right around that time, I had a dream. It had been six months since my mother died, and in the dream, I was told that I could visit her. I went up in a jet. She entered it mid-flight from the back of the plane and came down the aisle, beaming at me. She sat next to me and curled around me, never speaking, just smiling. I told her all about myself, about my childhood and about my love of books. She nodded and almost cooed, but she never spoke.

I felt love radiate from her, and I felt something strongly maternal flow from her. I almost expected her to count my fingers and toes! I had the realization that in the next life, we get to be the individual God created each of us to be, before our walls go up and cloak parts of our personhood.

Eventually I knew she had to leave. She quietly held my hand. Then she got up, walked back down the aisle, and disappeared. When I woke up, I felt almost as though I had had a visitation. I felt that I knew her suddenly, and I felt so very sorry that she could not bring down her own walls enough to know me in this life. For the first time, I felt grief. I cried for days.

Kit Kat took to climbing on me and kneading her paws into me as if she were nursing. She treated me as if I was her mother. I felt terribly protective. I felt her little claws and loved her and cried. I didn't think I could stand to lose her. I took her to a different vet.

"This cat does not have FIP," the vet proclaimed. If she did she'd be dead by now, and she certainly wouldn't be this hale and hearty." I consulted yet another vet who said the same.

"Do you mean I may have her for many years?" I asked this one.

"No reason why not."

Did Kit Kat ever have FIP? Probably not, though I have friends who believe love healed her. My maternalism slowly relaxed, and my grief about my mother turned into the dull ache it needed to be. Joe and I both adore Kit Kat, though she's partial to him; when he's in the room, I cease to exist. But that's okay. He's her rescuer, her fellow cat. I'm her mother object. We are thankful every day that she survived and walked back to us.

I learn from Kit Kat. Abandoned, she nevertheless chose the way she would live. I was abandoned, too, and I have worked through those issues and have gotten on with life with a fresh appreciation for my adopted family.

We live in a fallen world. Kittens are thrown into the wild by cruel people. Mothers can't always keep their babies. But there are also small miracles: Kit Kat finding us, my people finding me, Kit Kat insisting that she is ours, Joe losing his allergy, my meeting my mother in a vivid dream, Kit Kat's clean bill of health. These are the things for which I am grateful. These are the ways I know my Creator watches over us.

# Part of
# the Plan

*But ask now the beasts,*
*and they shall teach thee;*
*and the fowls of the air,*
*and they shall tell thee:*
*Or speak to the earth,*
*and it shall teach thee:*
*and the fishes of the sea*
*shall declare unto thee.*

—Job 12:7–8 (KJV)

# A Horse for Haley

### Catherine Madera

$\mathcal{T}$he stallion huddled in the corner of the small paddock, his crusty hide sagging from his bones. His owner had said the horse was a half-Arabian pinto, but I could barely make out the two-color coat beneath the muck. His hair was matted and mud-caked, his mane dirt-streaked. I approached cautiously, but the horse took no notice. He just picked list-lessly at a clump of hay. No wonder he's being offered for free, I thought. No one would want a horse like this.

"Free Horse." That's what my husband had scribbled down on a notepad along with a phone number, an offhand mention by a friend. It seemed like perfect timing—we were looking for a horse for our nine-year-old daughter, Haley. A year ago, when she was finally old enough to help take care of a horse and ride on her own, we had bought her a snow-white Welsh mare named Lady. She turned out to be the perfect horse for Haley—gentle, well-behaved, as comfortable walking in our town's Independence Day parade as she was roaming the nature trails around our farm. But Lady developed laminitis, a crippling condition. We had to put her down, and Haley was devastated. Our other horses were too big and spirited for her. She was using a friend's pony to complete her 4-H program, but I knew how badly she wanted a horse of her own and I'd prayed for an answer. "Free Horse?" There had to be a catch. ...

There was. On the phone, the man had told me the horse was a stallion, neglected and left to run wild by its previous owner. Already that told me the horse wasn't good for Haley, or any child. Stallions are naturally more aggressive than mares. Even if gelded, the horse was completely untrained. At eight years old, he might never come around. But my curiosity led me to the man's farm. I'd trained several horses. Perhaps I could nurse this stallion back to health, train him, then put him up for sale and use the money to get Haley a new horse. Since Lady had died, we had a stall available. Besides, I knew if I didn't take a chance on this horse, I was pretty sure no one else would. *Chance, a good name for a horse*, I thought.

The following weekend I brought Chance home. His weak back legs wobbled so much he could barely step into the horse trailer. I had to practically push him in.

The first thing I did was put him in a round pen, away from our other horses, and focus on getting some weight on him. I walked out to the pen twice a day to feed him. "Can I feed him, Mommy?" Haley asked.

"Not yet," I said. I needed to see how Chance would behave first.

After about three months of good food and care Chance regained his strength—and his attitude. I opened up his pen one morning and he burst out, tearing around the pasture in a panic. "Easy, son, easy," I said in a low soothing voice, but when I approached, he turned and bolted. I finally managed to get him back in his pen. Then he reared up and struck my shoulder with his hoof. I was all right, but frustrated. Horses aren't violent creatures; they'd rather flee than fight. Yet Chance always wanted to lash out. I figured he'd been abused; that's why he didn't trust people. Lord, how do I get him to trust me?

"Can I feed Chance?" Haley asked later. After that morning, I was especially emphatic in my response. How could I risk a horse hurting my daughter? "Absolutely not, Haley," I said. "You must not go anywhere near Chance. Is that understood? He's just too dangerous."

"I understand, Mom," Haley said, disappointment in her voice.

"Don't worry," I said. "We'll get you a horse soon."

I knew how curious Haley was about our new horse, but Chance was no Lady. The sooner I could train him, clean him up and sell him, the better.

A few weeks later, Chance had calmed down enough that I felt comfortable trying to groom him. When he saw me with brushes, he backed away and neighed loudly. "Shh, easy, son, easy." I laid my hand softly along his side and rubbed gently. The crust on his flanks wiped away to reveal his silky white coat spotted with deep mahogany patches. The thick bristles of the brush combed through his matted mane, untangling the long, white wisps. I could see his breathing slow, his eyes no longer wide and scared. "When was the last time someone groomed you like this?" I said. I took a step back when I was done, admiring my work.

"He's so beautiful, Mommy," Haley said. She stood at the edge of the pen, staring at Chance. I had to admit his coloring was quite striking. Maybe with some training he wouldn't be so hard to sell. One of the basics was getting Chance to walk into a trailer. He had done it when I brought him here, after all. But now Chance threw himself against the walls and struck out with his front hooves, behavior I had only read about in horse-training books that said some horses acted out like this when they were stressed in small spaces. It wasn't only dangerous for me; Chance could hurt himself. Then he bolted out of the trailer in a panic. What was I to do?

I remembered how well Chance had reacted when I groomed him. I couldn't be a taskmaster with this horse. He just needs a little kindness and consistency, I thought.

I took plenty of time training him to the trailer. Slow and steady, I'd lead him into the middle of the trailer, standing at his head, stroking his mane. My touch seemed to calm him. When I tied him down and left the trailer, he started to get antsy. But I noticed that as long as he could still see me, he stayed put. "No worries, pal, I'm right here," I said, and he quieted down. Progress, finally. *Thank You, Lord. This is going to take the two of us for sure.*

Meanwhile, Haley and I began a search for her horse. We went to check out a horse my friend heard about, only to discover it was lame. One we found in the paper seemed perfect, until we saw it in person and it towered over Haley. I searched on the Internet. More than a few times I'd catch Haley looking forlornly at pictures of Lady. "God knows the right horse for you," I assured her. But the look on her face said it all. She loved Lady and nothing could replace her.

It took months of work, but Chance made great strides. He could be loaded onto a trailer no problem—with or without another horse. He rarely bucked when I rode him. Instead of running off when I approached, he'd walk up to me in the field. He was well-behaved enough that I even let Haley help me groom him—something that had become Chance's favorite activity. Watching the care that she gave to Chance reminded me of the way she was with Lady. *God, Haley's still hurting*, I prayed. *Please help me find the right horse for her.* Once I sold Chance I could give that mission my full attention. All I needed was a few good pictures of him to put online.

"Haley, why don't you lead Chance around while I try to get a good shot," I said. Chance followed Haley around the pasture. "Can you get him to lift up his head?" I asked. Haley stroked Chance under the chin and he lifted his head.

I posted the photos online, anticipating some response. Chance was only eight, small, fairly well-trained, and the photos showed how handsome he'd become. But weeks later I hadn't received even one nibble. *Maybe if we get some pictures of Haley riding him . . .*

I stood in the pasture, watching as Haley guided Chance. Haley looked so happy in her riding helmet, her ponytail bobbing up and down as she pushed Chance to a trot and slowed to a stop. They looked so...natural.

For the next few weeks, as I waited anxiously for a buyer, Haley rode Chance around the farm. I kept a close eye on them, not ready to fully trust Chance yet. But he never gave Haley any trouble. Haley began feeding him and took over his care. I noticed he always nickered to her when she fed him.

"Why don't we take him out on the trail?" I said to Haley one day. I saddled up one of our horses, and Haley rode Chance. It was peaceful, quiet, only an occasional snort from the horses and their hooves crackling the fallen leaves that littered the trail. Just then, a guy on a dirt bike zoomed up. My horse backed away from the revving engine. I held the reins tightly, afraid he would bolt. I shot a terrified glance at Haley. How would Chance react? He didn't move a muscle. The dirt bike passed and Haley patted Chance on the side. "Good boy," she said.

His behavior amazed me. As the trail ride progressed, it began to dawn on me why Chance wasn't selling. And why I'd been so moved to give him a chance in the first place. *How could I have missed it, Lord?* Haley must have read my mind. "So, Mom," she said. "Chance can be my horse, can't he?"

"I think that was the plan all along," I said. We meandered along the trail back toward the farm, every clip clop of hooves next to me the sound of an answered prayer.

# A Little Lamb
*Janice Wolf*

*A* caravan of critters followed me as I trudged through the field on my feeding rounds: Noogie, a one-eyed llama; Puzzle, a three-legged bull-mastiff; and Oops, a blind black Lab. I appreciated the company, but couldn't ignore one glaring absence—Shiloh, my Anatolian shepherd. From the day I founded Rocky Ridge Refuge, she had always trotted by my side. But now in her old age, she seemed to lose interest in everything. All she did for the past few weeks was lie around the house with her head resting on her paws, and that just got me to brooding—How long before I end up doing the same thing? At forty-nine I wasn't as strong or as fit as I used to be either. They say fifty is the new forty, but I didn't think so. Some days I felt like Shiloh, an old dog that couldn't keep up anymore. I finished filling the troughs and headed to the house. *Better check on her,* I thought.

Helping neglected and abused animals had been my calling ever since I was a little girl, when I rescued an injured pelican I found near my home in Key West, Florida. After college I became a rehabilitation counselor, but my heart was with animals so I became a veterinarian technician. Finally, I rented fifteen acres in the Ozarks of northern Arkansas and opened Rocky Ridge, a place where I could care for special-needs animals and provide alternative, natural remedies to those who failed to get well with traditional veterinary medicine.

Shiloh was the first animal I brought to the refuge. She held down the home front as I worked three jobs just to support myself and the creatures we cared for. Shiloh welcomed all the animals I sheltered: from Lurch—an African Watusi with record-breaking, seven-foot-long, thirty-eight-inch-wide horns—to a zebra named Zebiscuit, an exotic pet that someone couldn't keep. Shiloh played in the yard with them, helped me shepherd the animals into the shelter at night and in bad weather. Most important, her sharp bark scared away coyotes, bobcats and other hungry predators lurking in the dense Ozark forest. In the past thirteen years, with Shiloh by my side, the refuge had grown to include fifty animals from all over the country, more than I could handle, I feared. *This place is as much hers as it is mine*, I thought. How will I do it all without her?

Shiloh barely stirred when I came through the door. Been a long time since she's greeted me. When a dog stops saying hello you know it's in trouble. I knelt beside her, dipping a spoon into her water dish and coaxing her to sip. Some of the water dribbled down her chest. She could barely manage three spoonfuls. Part of me wanted to admonish her—"C'mon old girl. I know you can!"—but I understood how she felt. Some days I want to give up too. *Lord, Shiloh and I both need You. More than ever.*

The ringing phone interrupted my thoughts, and I rushed to answer it. It was my friend Sandy. "Janice, could you take a newborn lamb?" she asked. "One of her legs was broken during birth, and the mother has rejected her." I had so many animals to care for already, but the lamb was getting weaker every minute she went without her mother's milk.

"Bring her as soon as you can," I said. I hung up the phone and found a warm, blanket to lay on the floor by Shiloh. "You're going to have a new roommate," I told her. She raised her head briefly, then lay it down again. There was a time when caring for another animal was as important to

Shiloh as it was to me. Dogs need a sense of purpose too. Had Shiloh lost that?

Sandy arrived and we put the lamb on the blanket. She was so tiny! Like a mound of mashed potatoes. "I'm going to name you Tater!" I said, warming a bottle of formula on the stove. I applied a cast to stabilize her leg. Then I pulled her close and tried to get her to drink. She didn't latch on, so I squeezed the bottle gently and sprayed some of the milk into her open mouth. She opened her eyes weakly and stuck out her little pink tongue. It took some fits and starts, but finally she caught on and began to nurse. I unfolded her legs and let her lean against me while she emptied the bottle. "Good, Tater, good," I said. Out of the corner of my eye I could see Shiloh staring at us. She caught me looking and put her head back down again.

Two mornings later, Tater was much stronger. She drained her bottle at breakfast and, for the first time, started hobbling around, exploring her surroundings. I looked on anxiously. What if her leg doesn't hold? Just then, Tater spied Shiloh. The little lamb bleated and began limping toward her. "No, no, sweetie," I said, reaching out and grabbing her. "Don't bother Shiloh." But the lamb strained against my grasp. *Let her go.* The words popped into my head suddenly. I released Tater but stayed close. Her tiny hooves made clicking sounds on the wooden floor as she awkwardly approached the dog. Shiloh raised her head. Finally, Tater reached her goal. With an awkward lunge, she pressed her small nose against Shiloh's. Shiloh inched her head back and looked up at me.

I scooped up Tater and carried her into the kitchen. She seemed content, following me around as I made breakfast, but when I sat down to eat, she headed toward Shiloh again, baaing at the top of her lungs. I scarfed down my toast and rushed after her. Oh, my! I burst out laughing. Shiloh was still lying down, but very much awake. Tater was standing behind her with her head nuzzled across the dog's thick furry neck. "Looks like you made a friend, Shiloh," I said. The lamb stayed there until I had to take Shiloh for her walk. I could hear Tater inside baaing pitifully as Shiloh slowly walked her usual small circle just outside the house. But when we got back, Shiloh ignored Tater, plopping down against the wall with her back to the lamb. *Poor Shiloh,* I thought. *She's exhausted. Am I asking too much of her?* I left to do my feeding rounds.

Piling up some hay for Lurch, my own fatigue set in. These acres seem bigger every day. I leaned against my pitchfork. It seemed like yesterday Shiloh was running alongside the others. I hoped Tater wasn't bothering her too much. I finished up and headed back. Tater would be hungry.

Sure enough, when I opened the door, there was Tater, waiting for me. But she wasn't alone. Shiloh was standing too, right behind her, up and alert—greeting me. "Why I never ... " I gasped. "What have you two ladies been up to?"

Tater followed me into the kitchen, seeking her warm bottle. Again, I was amazed to see Shiloh right behind her! She watched me as I pulled Tater's bottle from the fridge, placed it in a pan of water on the stove to warm up. "Now you're interested in your lamb?" I asked Shiloh. She wagged her tail and went over to her water and food dishes. I almost fainted when she started to eat and took a few laps of water. I sat down to feed Tater and Shiloh sidled up next to us.

*Okay, Lord, there's a message in here for me, isn't there?* I thought.

Every day, I'd find Shiloh walking around the house with Tater. When anyone came in, Shiloh stood between the lamb and the guest, protecting her until the visitor passed inspection. One spring day Tater went out for the first time. Shiloh walked out with her, watching her play. Tater ran over and the two rubbed noses. Shiloh couldn't keep up with Tater, but she kept an eye on her, tongue hanging out happily. Shiloh was a working dog again. She had rediscovered her purpose.

Later that year Shiloh grew weak again. It broke my heart to see her try to stand when Tater nudged her. Shiloh's days were numbered.

She passed away peacefully two months after Tater arrived. I grieved, but was comforted by the memory of how proudly she'd walked beside her lamb. She'd been ready to go two months ago, but hadn't stopped working until Tater was strong enough to be on her own. God used a lamb to give new purpose to an old dog's life—and to mine. I'm not caring for these animals by myself after all. And that will keep me going for a long, long time.

# All Mine

### Marion Bond West

*M*arion, why don't you get another cat?" a friend suggested one day last spring. "You loved Minnie."

"That's exactly why I don't want another one now," I said. "That cat broke my heart. I'm not ready to go through something like that again."

Two years had passed since we put down Minnie at age seventeen. I still missed her every day. I missed her spying out our living room curtains at the bird feeder, running to rub against my legs every time she heard the false promise of the electric can opener. There were those luminous yellow eyes blinking "hello" to Gene and me when we walked in the door, and the little thump she made jumping up on our bed at night and settling down contentedly between us. I missed that thump. But most of all, there were those recurring dreams I had.

"Besides," I told my friend, "things are easier now. No more cat hair all over everything. And Gene and I can take last-minute trips without feeling guilty." No, it wouldn't make any sense to get another cat. End of story.

Not quite. That night I had the dream again. Cats of all kinds trailing me as if I were the Pied Piper of tuna. *Stop it, Marion!* I told myself in the morning. *Dream cats aren't real cats. They never die and leave you grieving.*

I sat down with the newspaper at breakfast. An announcement jumped out at me. "Pet Adoption Day at the Oconee Library. Saturday 10 AM. Give an Abandoned Pet a Home."

*Abandoned*. That's got to be one of the saddest words in the English language. I said a quick prayer. "Please, may all those poor, lonely, frightened animals find a home." To myself, I added, *But not with me. Not until I'm ready. Not until this pain stops.*

Saturday morning I set out to do my usual errands. First stop, the supermarket. Or so I thought. Inexplicably, I found myself taking the turnoff to the library instead. I'm just going to see if any new books have arrived.

The Oconee County Animal Control van was parked opportunistically near the sidewalk leading to the library entrance. I marched past the dogs in their cages, my eyes focused straight ahead. *Don't even look.*

I nearly fell over a table set up by the library door. A woman sat there smiling. Beside her was a small animal carrier.

"Can I help you?" she asked.

"No, thanks," I said. *Keep walking, Marion. This is dangerous.*

Meow! The sound emanated from the carrier. I stopped in my tracks. "Looking for a new friend?" the woman asked.

"Not me. Not after my last cat died." There. I'd said it. Now it was safe for me to peek through the door of the pet carrier. One look and I'd be on my way.

A pair of large amber eyes like polished marbles gazed back at me. What took you so long? they seemed to say, and for a crazy moment, I thought the cat had been expecting me. *Marion! No more cats.* But she was so petite and delicate, long-haired, black and white. "Hi, girl," I whispered. I touched her nose through the wire door. She began to purr as though a tiny switch had been turned on.

"How long has she been at the shelter?" I asked.

"She was dropped off a few weeks ago with three newborn kittens," the woman said. "The kittens died. We had a hard time taking them from her. She was a good little mama cat."

"Oh, girl," I said, "don't you worry, somebody nice will come and adopt you." The cat pressed her head against my hand, and I couldn't resist asking, "Can I take her out of the carrier?"

"Sorry," the woman said. "Only if you're thinking of taking her."

I wasn't.

I sat on the sidewalk and watched the cat wash her fur. *Lord, this pretty little cat deserves a good home. Please find someone who is ready to love her.*

People stopped by to see the dogs and fill out adoption forms. I was content just to sit with the little black-and-white cat. If I could purr, I might have. I checked my watch. I'd been sitting here almost an hour! "We're not that busy right now," the woman from the shelter said. "Suppose I let you hold her." She unlatched the carrier door.

"Come here, girl," I said. The cat reached out and put a tiny white paw on my hand. She paused, looked up and meowed. Cats can be aloof. This one acted very familiar. I lifted her out, and she nestled against my neck, all fuzzy and warm. *Purrrrr.*

"What would you name her?" the woman asked.

It just popped out of my mouth. "Girl Friend." Where on earth had that come from? "But there's no way I can take her," I said quickly. "I'm not ready."

"Too bad. She's really taken to you."

Girl Friend rubbed her cheek against mine. I didn't want to fall in love. That's the thing about love, though, you can't decide on it, and I couldn't deny it. I was officially in love, ready or not. *Okay, Lord, I know I asked You to find this cat a home. But this isn't what I had in mind.*

I put the cat back in the carrier and filled out an adoption form. The woman told me it would take a few days to be approved. "Sit tight, Girl Friend," I said. "I'll be back for you."

"I've found us a new cat," I told Gene when I got home. He gave me a sidelong glance, but didn't say anything. For the next three days all I thought about was that cat, her nose pressing into my hand, her purr that vibrated through my whole arm when I petted her. Finally the woman from the shelter called. "Your adoption application went through. She's all yours."

In no time Girl Friend was exploring our house, making herself at home. She investigated under the beds, among the closet shelves, inside the grand piano. Then she ran to the sink and meowed until I turned on the faucet for her to drink.

I went to bed that first night fairly confident that I wouldn't dream of cats. I was just drifting off when I felt a familiar little thump on the bed. Girl Friend padded up the covers and snuggled down between us. *Purrrrr.* Blink, went her amber eyes. And to think I had almost missed out on this! All along I had said I wasn't ready. For two years I grieved for Minnie. Sometimes we can get lost in our own pain. But there's always a way out. Even if we don't see it. I'd asked the Lord to give Girl Friend what she needed. He gave me exactly what I needed too.

# The Turtles of Topsail Island

*Jean Beasley*

My brother, Richard, saw it first. "Jean!" he shouted, running up toward our little vacation beach house. "There's something huge coming out of the ocean!" The moon wasn't quite full that summer night on Topsail Island back in 1970. But it was pretty close. My husband, Fred, and I had fallen in love with the beaches of Topsail back in 1970, on our honeymoon. We'd vacationed there ever since, and had recently bought this beach house. I squinted down toward the waves. An animal the size of a truck engine was making its way up the beach, right for our house. It was past midnight, but I ran inside and woke up the kids. We all gathered on the deck.

"What is it, Mom?" Karen asked. Eight that summer, she was my youngest and every bit the nature lover I'd been at that age.

"It's a turtle," I said. "A sea turtle." I'd seen the posters put up by the National Marine Fisheries Service. Sea turtles were a threatened species. The females lumbered ashore to lay their eggs.

She came to a halt right at our porch steps and began digging with her back flippers. Sand flew through the air, smacking against the porch. One by one the family got enough of the spectacle and headed back to bed. Not Karen and me. Wrapped in blankets, we watched until two in the morning, when the turtle finally finished her task and crawled back into the thundering waves.

Early the next morning Karen and I were down in the sand, examining the spot where we knew the eggs were buried. "How long do you think it'll take them to hatch, Mom?"

"Let's find out," I said. We called the North Carolina Wildlife Resources Commission, but they had no record of turtles nesting on Topsail Island. Finally, we found a government pamphlet that gave us some answers. What we'd seen was a loggerhead—one of seven species of sea turtles, all of which were either endangered or threatened. Sea turtles live their entire lives in the ocean, except for when the females, traveling hundreds, or even thousands of miles, somehow return to the exact beaches where they hatched decades earlier to lay eggs of their own.

Female loggerheads laid several nests, coming back to shore repeatedly over the course of a few weeks. Karen and I walked up and down the beach, looking for trenches in the sand like the one our turtle had made (they're so big that people sometimes mistake them for bulldozer tracks). We found a bunch, but we'd learned that as little as one turtle in ten thousand makes it to adulthood.

Nests take about sixty days to hatch. Karen and I were back home in Ohio by the time the babies in "our" nest saw the light of day. The first thing we did when we returned the next year was check on it. There wasn't much left to see—just the vaguest indentation in the sand where we knew it had been. How many babies had made it down to the water?

"I wish we could have been here to help, Mom," Karen said, a little sad. So did I.

Summer by summer we learned more about the turtles—and about how to help them. We swept over the trenches left by mothers so their nests would be undisturbed. When hatching time came we dug roads in the sand that the babies could follow down to the surf. Sometimes we found stragglers from a night-time hatching. We'd put them into the water and say a prayer for them as they winged their way toward deeper water. We kept track of the nests we found and reported them to wildlife officials. Word spread about this strange mother-daughter turtle-finding team. We got calls about injured turtles that washed up on Topsail's twenty-six miles of beach. Fishing nets and speedboats can be a menace to them. Turtles hit by propellers were one of the most common victims on Topsail's beaches. There was little that Karen and I could do for these animals.

Not that Karen didn't have things in her life besides turtles. In 1990—the same year that Fred retired and we moved to Topsail permanently—she graduated from college and got a position with a Charlotte public relations firm. We were incredibly proud of her—what mother wouldn't be? And probably more excited about her new life than she was.

But then something terrible happened. Like so many terrible things it started out small—just a nagging cough. It wouldn't stop nagging her. Karen saw our family doctor. She had leukemia.

"The more rest she gets," the doctor said, "the better chance she has." Karen gave up her dream job and moved back into the beach house with Fred and me.

Orders to rest or not, Karen stayed busy. It was the height of the nesting season. Mother turtles were laying eggs up and down the beach.

"That's the third call we've got this morning about the same turtle nest," Karen said one morning, exasperated. "Mom, we need to get this thing more organized."

So the Topsail Island Turtle Project was officially born. Karen lectured at schools and libraries, explaining the vital role that sea turtles play in the ocean's ecosystem. Turtles are a bellwether species. Their disappearance means more than just no more turtles. It means our oceans are dying. How, Karen asked, could we sit back and let these animals slip into nonexistence before our eyes?

Extinction is a big word. Most of us don't want to think about what it means. Extinction is a full stop. There's no coming back. It's permanent, irreversible. It takes courage to imagine something that large—that terrible. But Karen had that courage. She knew what it meant to face up to endings, even if I was still struggling to accept her worsening illness.

"Mom," she said to me one day as we were looking out the kitchen window at the late autumn light, "you know they signed me up for a life-insurance policy when I was working. I don't want my illness to be the center of my life. I want the turtles to be the center of it. If I don't make it, I want you to use that money for them."

*If I don't make it.* The words hung in the air. Karen and I didn't talk about death. It was too painful for me. But she cared too much about the turtles to risk my not knowing her wishes.

"Okay, Karen," I said. "I promise."

Late one evening in 1991 Karen and I got a phone call that a big female had come ashore a few miles down the beach from us. Karen's illness had been running her hard of late—harder than usual—but she refused to let her disease get in the way of helping those turtles. So we got into the car and drove down to the spot where the caller had indicated.

The telltale furrow in the sand was easy to see in the moonlight. Karen and I found a spot close enough to the nesting turtle to keep an eye on it, but far enough away that we wouldn't disturb it. Next to the moment when the newly hatched turtles make their mad dash to the waves, nesting can be the most dangerous moment in mama turtle's life.

But not with Karen around. "Do you want to go home and get some rest, Karen?" I realized how foolish the question was before it was out of my mouth.

"Don't worry, Mom. I'll get some rest later. As soon as she's safe." It was 2:00 AM before the turtle had laid the last of her eggs and slipped back into the sea. Karen went home and slept in. The next day, she felt too ill to go out. *No, God, no*, I prayed. *I'm not ready to lose Karen.*

Two days later, Karen slipped away peacefully, just a few months before her thirtieth birthday.

I plunged into helping the turtles with more energy than ever, channeling a grief that seemed too much for me to bear. Karen was gone—at least from the earth. But her work on behalf of the earthly creatures she cared for most went on.

In 1995, four years after Karen's death, a forty-pound immature loggerhead turtle washed up on the beach at North Topsail Island with severe injuries, most likely caused by a boat propeller. Greg Lewbart, a doctor at North Carolina State University College of Veterinary Medicine, agreed to look at him. "This turtle is lucky you found him when you did," Dr. Lewbart told me. "He's also lucky that his braincase wasn't broken or his optic nerve severed by the propeller that hit him."

I decided to call him Lucky.

We fixed up Lucky with a discarded fiberglass tank, and he ended up spending eighteen months with us. When his wounds were finally healed, some Topsail Island Turtle Project volunteers and I carried him down to the sea. "So long, Lucky," I said, as he slowly flapped out to sea. "May the Lord watch over you."

I had seen plenty of turtles by then, but only in passing. Lucky was the first Topsail sea turtle I really got to know personally. There's something uniquely painful and rewarding about taking in a wild creature, caring for it, coming to know it as an individual and setting it free again. You put so much love and worry into the animal...and then you place it right back in harm's way.

Of course, that's what every parent does as well. No one knew that better than I did.

In the days after Lucky left us, I couldn't get Karen's words out of my mind. Help the turtles. To really help them I needed—the turtles needed—a turtle hospital. The Karen Beasley Sea Turtle Rescue and Rehabilitation Center opened its doors in the fall of 1997. Since then we've rehabilitated and released more than 150 sick and injured sea turtles. Some stay with us for just a few days. Others spend months, even years here. But for all of these animals, there eventually comes a moment when I have to tell them good-bye, when I have to give them back to the ocean, and back to God.

It's never easy. But there's no time that I feel closer to God—or to Karen—than when I place one of these turtles in the waves and watch it swim off to make its ancient way in the world. Sea turtles are just one of the world's many endangered species. But they're my species—the one I've dedicated my heart and my life to helping, just like Karen did.

By chance or, perhaps, by something more, a mother turtle picked my daughter and me on that moonlit summer night so many years ago, when she crawled out of the sea, right up to our doorstep on Topsail Island. Yes, God does have a way of getting your attention.

# Bambo

*Byron Davenport*

*I* lived in a big empty house, set way back from the road and fenced on ten acres. It was just me and my Brittany spaniel, Levi. That's the way I wanted it. I was raised in church, but as a youngster I saw that some of those people who were nice and all smiles on Sundays could be pretty mean the rest of the week. I stopped going and didn't intend to start up again. I used to be married—twice—and even had kids. But both women left me, and they pretty much gave the same reason: "You're hardheaded and hard-hearted, and you'll never change." My daughter Brandi stayed on, at least until she met Mr. Right and moved out. My dad had passed on, but Momma lived just down the road.

One Saturday four years ago I was in my Dodge Ram, passing by a town named Arcade. I had to slam on the brakes when a speeding car ahead of me smacked right into a doe and kept on going. The deer was dead on impact. But a scrawny fawn stood there on shaky legs, looking right at me. I felt a tug in my chest, kind of like when a fish grabs your line after a long day of no bites. I hadn't felt something like that for a long time, and I wanted no part of it now. Still, that fawn looked right at me. *I didn't kill your mother*, I thought. Then I hit the gas and took off. But I glanced in my rearview mirror, and my mind snapped a picture of the little guy standing there all alone.

Back home I couldn't get that picture out of my mind. After about an hour, I got into the pickup and went back to the spot, feeling stupid, to be honest. I mean, I'm the kind of guy who hunts deer instead of rescuing them. But the little fellow was still there, almost like he'd been waiting for me. I cut the ignition and got out. The fawn hesitated before taking a step toward me. I stuck out my hand, palm up. He took another step and laid his head right in my hand. And that weird feeling in my chest came back. I bent down and scooped up the fawn. He couldn't have weighed more than four or five pounds.

A name popped into my head, but I didn't say it. Not yet. I waited till the fawn met my dog. "Levi, this here's Bambo," I said. Levi wagged his stubby tail, went right over and started licking the fawn's face. Right then I knew Bambo would move in.

I set up a king-size mattress and a pillow in one of the empty bedrooms. I laid Bambo down right in the middle. He folded up his legs and pulled himself into a circle. I went to dig out an old baby bottle and some milk. He slurped down bottle after bottle. I soon discovered Bambo had broad tastes: He liked Lucky Charms, muscadines, apples, oatmeal pie and peppermint candy. But his favorite thing of all was Yoo-Hoo.

We established a routine. Levi would curl up on the bed next to Bambo each night. I'd leave a snack and say good-night. Sometimes Bambo got up in the middle of the night for the snack. Or he'd clomp into my room and chew on my hair till I woke. I'd take him out back and stay on the porch with the light on while Bambo found his favorite tree.

Bambo grew antlers and put on more than a hundred pounds that first year. But he was still gentle and loving. By then I'd taken to letting him roam around outside when I was home. My property abuts the grounds of an elementary school. Bambo and the kids became fast friends. They loved petting him, and he loved the treats they brought.

I should have seen it coming, I guess. But I didn't want to. The letter from the school officials. It made sense—mating season was coming, and

Bambo might hurt some of the kids by accident. Deer can be testy, and they're strong. Bambo had to go, they said.

I met with a couple of guys from the white-tailed deer research facility at the University of Georgia. They're well-known in academic research circles. It's a top-notch place. The deer they study aren't hurt in any way, and there's nothing invasive. "You can come visit Bambo," they said. Even bring him treats. I didn't want to let Bambo go. But I knew I had to.

Early in the morning—the sun wasn't even up yet—in October 2003 I went into Bambo's room and climbed into bed with him and Levi. I wanted so bad to tell him that he was leaving that day, and explain why it had to be. But words wouldn't come. Just a kind of sick feeling in my stomach. Bambo looked at me, and I could swear he knew.

Momma came by later, and a few other folks. When the university's truck pulled up, I blinked hard and fast, trying to keep my tears inside. Bambo climbed into the back of the truck. Levi looked from me to the deer and back. He didn't know what was happening to his friend. Momma reached out to hold me, and I grabbed onto her something fierce. The truck rolled down the driveway, and I made terrible noises crying. Levi followed me into the house, into Bambo's bedroom, where we sat together on the mattress. An empty Yoo-Hoo bottle sat on the floor nearby.

Bambo's leaving was the last straw. All of a sudden I could see inside myself, all the things I'd promised never to look at again. My two divorces, my kids leaving, my dad dying. All that loss and pain was still there, waiting to be dealt with.

Instead, I tried to keep busy and forget how much my heart hurt. But I couldn't. Nothing made sense. I didn't even bother getting out of bed some days. I'd lie there all day long staring out the window. Deer hunting was over for sure now.

Momma came over with a book called *The Message*. It's the Bible in plain English. I didn't pick it up once. Brandi came over one day with my grandson Joshua. I barely spoke to them. Joshua was walking around my room and wandered over to the window. He stared out it. Just like I spent my time staring out it.

The very next day I noticed Joshua had left a handprint on the glass. First thing I'd noticed in a while. I got up and went over to the window. Slowly I covered the print with my own hand, being careful not to rub it off. I just needed to touch it.

When I did, something washed over me. Right there I fell to my knees and cried out, "God, can You hear me? Do You see me? Please, Sir, I can't help myself. For the first time ever, I can't help myself." And if I couldn't even help myself, what use would I be to my grandson, my kids, my momma?

Whether you believe it or not, God answered me. Imagine you are in the darkest night. A never-ending blackness. And then suddenly the sun pops out, so bright you have to squint. That's what it felt like. I knew God had heard. I knew he was there for me. I grabbed the book Momma had given me and opened it. She'd written me a little note and marked a Scripture for me to read in Psalms: "Heart-shattered lives ready for love don't for a moment escape God's notice."

God knew my heart had been shattered one time too many. He brought me Bambo, so I could love again. So I could live. And that day, standing at the window, was the start of a new life, a new me. It wasn't an easy path. I'm still nothing close to perfect. But it was the right path.

I visit Bambo once in a while, bringing along some peppermint as a treat. He's doing fine in his new home. And I'm doing fine in my old one.

# Lady & Alexander

### Cheryl Christensen

You might call my son, Alexander, a Mayberry throwback, as in the old feel-good TV show *The Andy Griffith Show*. Skinny, sandy-haired and freckle-faced, he even has an old-fashioned look. You're more likely to find him hunting for tadpoles than playing the latest video game, and he'd rather be walking through the woods than the mall. He rescues injured blue jays and robins and brings them to wildlife rehabilitators. I've seen him pry a chipmunk from the jaws of a neighborhood cat and nurse the little creature back to health.

His compassion amazes me. Still, I couldn't help worrying about him. Alexander seemed so different from the other boys in our suburban Atlanta neighborhood, like he didn't fit in somehow. I bit my nails in the bleachers at Little League games, watching him chase after bugs instead of balls. I sat anxiously in the church gym, hoping that for once someone would pass him the basketball. I signed him up for theater groups and music lessons, hoping to connect him to his passion, whatever that might be. I prayed, *Dear God, please help Alexander find his place in your world.* Then I'd go back to searching for just the right extracurricular activity for my son, the one he'd excel in.

Nothing clicked. Until Alexander met the volunteers from Small Dog Rescue in the parking lot of our pet-supply store. He peppered them with questions about dog care and training, and asked about the characteristics of different breeds—the kind of interest I wished he'd shown in his schoolwork.

Although at ten he was two years shy of the minimum age requirement to volunteer, he won over the director. Alexander went through orientation and training, and soon he was spending four hours every Saturday in front of the store, greeting shoppers and talking to them about the dogs available for adoption. I'd drop him off at noon and when I picked him up in the late afternoon he would be full of stories about this pup or that.

Sometimes he brought home dogs to foster while they awaited their "forever" homes. "They won't be any trouble, Mom. I promise," he said. It was true—I never had to remind him to feed, water or walk them. Alexander researched dog care on the Internet and checked out every book on dog breeds and behavior the library had. My son had found his passion, all right. I thought my prayers had been answered.

Then one afternoon as soon as I arrived to pick him up, Alexander announced, "Mom, I want to foster Lady. No one else wants her."

One look at the dog by his side, and I knew why. This wasn't a teacup poodle or Pomeranian or any of the dainty purebreds that were quickly snatched up. This was a 60-pound mutt, with wiry blond fur and gangly legs. She quivered not with fear, like some abandoned dogs, but with a barely contained energy. The next thing I knew she leapt at me, her paws hitting me square on the chest, knocking me off kilter as she planted a big, slobbery kiss on my face.

"Alexander, I don't think she'll fit in at our house," I said. Much as his four sisters—Alexander's right in the middle—loved to play with the dogs he brought home, I could imagine they wouldn't be so excited about this big hyper mutt getting into their things.

"Lady has nowhere to go," he said. "She's already been at two homes, and they can't keep her. Please, Mom, let me foster her. I'll do all the work." He looked at me pleadingly.

I relented. "Okay, but remember, she'll be your responsibility."

But by then he was already chasing Lady around the parking lot.

Lady was fun, lovable even, but there were plenty of problems. She bounded over our kitchen table, dishes flying in her wake. She had an inexplicable interest in our laundry, especially the towels. She jumped onto the family room couch and dashed away, a brand-new throw pillow in her teeth.

"Lady, no!" I cried, every time she misbehaved. She cocked her head quizzically, not understanding why I was upset.

Alexander seemed almost as oblivious to Lady's mischief-making as she was. "Mom, isn't Lady smart?" he marveled. "She catches on really fast when I'm training her. And whenever there's something new in the house, she always sniffs it out."

One day she chomped right through our telephone wires. Alexander sat us all down—my husband, our girls and me—and explained, "Lady only did that because she's teething. She can't help it, but I'll do my best to distract her with toys." Try telling that to the phone company, I thought.

Every Saturday, Alexander brushed Lady and brought her to adoption day, championing her cause to anyone who walked by. Week after week there were no takers. Yet my son never lost hope. "God, please help Lady find the right home," I would hear him praying every night before bed.

The months dragged on, and still Lady wasn't placed with a new owner. I couldn't bring myself to dash my son's hopes, but I had to face facts: This dog was unadoptable. If we were going to be stuck with Lady, though, her behavior would have to improve. I confided my dilemma to the director of Small Dog Rescue, and asked if she could recommend a doggy boot camp.

Right away she thought of Mac. He'd started the K-9 unit at the police department in nearby DeKalb County. Now retired, Mac volunteered as a law enforcement consultant, scouting potential police dogs, often at local shelters. I called him and told him about Lady. He agreed to take a look at her. Alexander was thrilled. "This is it, Mom," he said. "This is what Lady's been waiting for." If only I could be so sure.

He put Lady into her crate and we drove to a park where Mac would evaluate her. Alexander sat in the back seat, beside Lady's crate, unusually quiet.

"You okay?" I asked.

"Just wondering what Mac's looking for," he said. Then he brightened and turned to Lady. "You're gonna do great," he said. "I just know it."

Mac shook hands with Alexander. "So, this is Lady," Mac said, scratching her between the ears. His friendliness put us all at ease. He showed Lady a rolled towel, taped on the outer edges so it looked like a large terry cloth hot dog. He held it above his head. Lady leapt high into the air to snatch it. Then Mac took the towel and hid it behind his back. Lady didn't hesitate. She circled him and seized it as adroitly as she stole things from my laundry basket.

"This dog has one strong prey drive," Mac said. For canine law enforcement work, he explained, an instinct to seek prey with single-minded focus is critical. Prey drive, agility, strength, size and a keen sense of smell enable police dogs to perform tasks that no human or machine could match. "Only a few dogs meet the criteria for police work," Mac said. "Lady's a natural."

Alexander practically glowed, he was so proud of Lady. The look on his face said it all: See, I knew she was special!

"If it's okay with you, Alexander, I'll take Lady," Mac said. "I'll bring her to the police academy and have her tested. My guess is she'll make a great explosives- or narcotics-sniffing dog."

Alexander bit his lip and nodded. "Can I say good-bye to her?"

"Of course," Mac said. "Why don't you take her over to my truck? She'll be more comfortable with you leading her."

Lady walked calmly beside Alexander on her leash. "Sit," he said, when they got to the truck. Lady sat. Alexander rewarded her with a treat and patted her on the head. "Good girl." He gave her one last hug. Then it was time to step aside and let Mac put her into the truck.

Alexander and I sat in our car, and watched them drive away. Tears streamed down my son's cheeks. "I know I did the right thing, but I'll miss her, Mom," he said. "I love her."

"I know, Alexander." I put my arms around him and hugged him tightly. "And I love you." As I held my son, my own eyes moistened. I loved his compassion and intelligence, his patience and maturity.

Not that I wouldn't ever worry about my son again (that's what moms do), but I knew I didn't need to. Alexander never stopped believing there was a greater plan for that impossible-to-place dog, long after everyone else had given up. A boy with that kind of faith would discover his own God-given gifts just fine. In fact, I think he already has.

# Kat Albrecht, Pet Detective

*Kat Albrecht*

*T*hat's right, I'm a real-life pet detective. Surprised? Don't be. Most people think of Jim Carrey's wacky *Ace Ventura* movies when they hear "pet detective." But I really do help people locate their missing pets. I've got hundreds of stories of finding animals whose owners thought they were lost forever. For me, though, the most miraculous journey was the one that led me to pet detective work in the first place.

I had two distinct childhood dreams: to be a cop like Angie Dickinson on *Police Woman* and to go on incredible adventures with my dog, like the characters in the *Big Red* book series. Pretty far-fetched for a girl growing up in industrial Fresno, California. At nineteen, I took a job as a 911 police dispatcher. Naturally, I had a dog.

Somewhere in my twenties, though, things took a wrong turn. Like a bloodhound hot on the trail can suddenly lose a scent, I woke up one day and realized I'd lost my way. I was thirty now, and the job that once had seemed like a stepping-stone to being a cop had become a prison. Every time I put on my headset, the calls poured in—a burglary, a drug overdose, a car wreck. I'd been so well trained to push aside my feelings and focus on getting the facts that nothing got to me anymore. Not screams for help, not shots fired, not even the terror-frayed voice of a parent reporting a missing child.

Maybe it was holding back my emotions that left me with this emptiness, this sense of disconnection. Maybe it was taking information from desperate people and never knowing what became of them. It was time, I decided, to get more directly involved in solving cases, helping people.

I completed the police academy and trained my two dogs, my Weimaraner, Rachel, and bloodhound, A. J. I moved to Santa Cruz and worked for a local police department, using Rachel to sniff out evidence on homicide cases and A. J. to track down fleeing criminals and missing persons. We were a good team, and we started to make headlines: "Dog Helps Crack Murder Case." "Bloodhound Locates Lost Alzheimer's Sufferer." "Detective Dog Nabs Robbery Suspect."

One afternoon a woman who'd read about us in the paper called me at the station. "Can you use your dogs to help me find my cat, Taffy? She's been missing for two days now," she said, her voice breaking. "I don't know what else to do."

Reflexively I took on the businesslike tone of my dispatcher days. "I'm sorry, ma'am. Search dogs are specifically trained to ignore the scent of cats and dogs so they can better locate people. I'm not able to use my dogs to help you."

Besides, wasn't my work looking for people, not pets who'd wandered off? Of course, I usually left crying relatives or victims to other officers so I could locate a piece of bedding or a toothbrush from which my dogs could pick up the scent of the person we were searching for. Then it was just me and my dog focusing all our energy on the trail.

Relatives embraced loved ones we found. Other cops celebrated an arrest. I fed chunks of cheddar cheese to my dog and cooed, "Good boy" or "Good girl."

Hard to beat the thrill of another job well done. Still, my favorite part of the day was bedtime, reading my Bible with Rachel curled up beside me and A. J. snoring at my feet. I never felt more connected to God's world.

One spring evening in 1996, the unthinkable happened. And it happened to me this time. A. J. ran off. I dashed between the towering redwood trees behind my cabin, Rachel barking in alarm from the yard (by then she was retired from tracking). "A. J.!" I called out, stumbling over a fallen trunk buried in moss. I prayed between shallow breaths.

*Calm down!* I commanded myself. Don't let your emotions get in the way. But it was no use. If I didn't find A. J., a part of me would forever remain in these dark woods calling his name.

Without A. J., I couldn't go any deeper into the woods without getting lost. Kea. I have to get Kea to look for him. Kea was my friend Jeanne's search dog, and she and A. J. had been on many a late-night mission together. I raced back to my cabin and called my friend. Within minutes, Kea was heading down the road in front of my cabin, sniffing out my A. J.

Suddenly Kea veered onto a private drive. She led me down a hill toward a cabin. On the front porch was a big wet bloodhound sniffing at a stack of boxes.

"A. J.!" He lifted his head and wagged his tail. I ran to my dog and buried my face in the heavy folds of skin along his neck, rubbing his chest the way he liked. "You naughty boy, you scared me half to death," I said.

Nestled in my cabin that night with A. J. and Rachel, I found myself thinking of the woman who'd called me years earlier asking me to look for her cat. Now I knew what it felt like to lose an animal you love. Why hadn't I helped that woman? Had she ever found her pet? What if I could still help others like her by training a dog to search for lost pets?

The search dog community considered tracking lost pets a waste of a good dog. But I knew dogs were used to find bombs, drugs, food, minerals, even termites. Why shouldn't a dog be trained to help people find pets who in every sense of the word were part of the family? How could I pass by another hand-scrawled "lost pet" poster flapping on a telephone pole, knowing that maybe there was a way I could help?

I trained Rachel to be my first pet detective. I printed flyers and handed them out to pet stores and veterinarians.

One of those vets gave my number to a man named Mike. His husky, Sky, had taken off into the forest after getting hit by a car. I brought Rachel out to the spot where Mike had seen his dog last. A light rain was falling. Rain enhances scent particles, so I was optimistic. "Do you want to work?" I asked Rachel, just as I used to before we started an evidence search. I slipped an orange vest over Rachel matching the one I wore reading "Lost Pet Rescue" and held up a piece of Sky's bedding. "Take scent," I said.

Rachel was off in an instant, heading into the Santa Cruz mountains. For more than an hour, she was hot on the trail. Then she abruptly stopped at a train trestle suspended over a canyon. She'd lost the scent.

I think I was more disappointed than Mike when I finally suggested he continue searching in the woods near the train tracks. I reluctantly headed for work. I went over the search again and again in my mind. Rachel had done her best. Still, I hated to think I had given someone false hope. Maybe this pet detective thing wasn't such a hot idea after all.

That night Mike called. "I found Sky!" he practically shouted. "I kept calling his name and he came out of the woods right where you suggested I look. I never would have ended up there if it weren't for you and Rachel. I can't thank you enough."

It worked! My crazy idea had actually helped someone! I felt a rush that was more intense than when I caught a criminal or found a missing person, even.

I couldn't wait to get that rush again. So I was hesitant to get involved when a woman named Marilyn called. She'd found some fur and blood on her street and believed a coyote had killed her cat Pippi. What was the point of searching for a pet who was most likely already dead?

"I'm not sure what I can do to help you since..."

"Please," said Marilyn, "couldn't you just come out and take a look?"

How could I refuse? By the time I got to Marilyn's house, her other cat, Muffin, had gone missing too.

From Rachel's tracking, it seemed likely the bloodstain was from Pippi. Marilyn nodded solemnly when I told her. "What about Muffin?" she asked.

I gave Rachel a tuft of fur Muffin had shed. Rachel took scent and immediately headed east. We broke into a jog, Marilyn falling slightly behind. Rachel cut away from the road and loped up a steep embankment toward an open field. She had her nose up high, and I scrambled to keep up. We hit an area littered with gravel. I slipped and dropped the leash. Rachel raced ahead, her tail a wiggling blur.

"Did you see?" shouted Marilyn behind me.

"See what?" I asked, getting back to my feet.

"Muffin!" Marilyn said. "Rachel just flushed her out of the field."

We followed Muffin's trail back to Marilyn's house, where the black and orange calico was sitting nonchalantly in the driveway. I fed Rachel her cheese reward. Marilyn scooped up Muffin. "You saved her life," she said. "But Pippi...."

Marilyn's voice trailed off, and she burst into tears. Just like so many family members on my missing person cases. Except this time something was different. This time I found myself crying too.

I said the first thing that came to mind. "I'm sure Pippi's with the Lord now." Marilyn nodded, her tears slowing a bit. I told her about the day A. J. disappeared. We talked about our faith. I couldn't remember ever discussing anything so personal with someone on the job before. Marilyn gave me a hug good-bye.

I was still thinking about her as I settled into bed with my dogs and my Bible that night. What had happened to that calm, detached cop persona I'd developed all those years ago as a dispatcher? If I let my feelings show, wouldn't they get in the way of my helping people? A. J. stirred at my feet. I opened the Bible and my eyes fell on a verse in Romans. "Rejoice with those who rejoice; Weep with those who weep."

All my years as a cop I'd never wept as I had with Marilyn that afternoon. Yet sharing my feelings—and my faith—with her had brought her some comfort, I was sure of it.

"God, are You trying to tell me this is my true calling?" Even as I spoke the words, I knew the answer. I had never felt so connected before, not only to my work and to my dogs, but to other people who love their pets as much as I do.

That's the reason I'm a real-life pet detective, and why you shouldn't be so surprised.

# The Gift of a Happy Memory

*Renie Szilak Burghardt*

*T*here is an old homestead in my neighborhood, with a weathered farmhouse, surrounded by rolling fields dotted with oak and hickory trees, encircled by a forest of more hickory and oak trees, and blessed with a small, winding creek that flows at the bottom of the field. Although the homestead had seen good days, with children thriving in the homey, country environment, it had been sadly neglected in the past few years, especially after the passing of my friend and neighbor, Anne. After Anne died, her husband, Dan, in his sixties, went to live with his son and family in St. Louis, and their trips to the old homestead had gotten scarce. Until Dan's family decided that a family reunion on the Old Home Place would be just the perfect setting for Dan's upcoming birthday, since he had become somewhat depressed over being away from it.

So it was a pleasant surprise to hear that they were planning this reunion, last spring. Dan's two sons, their wives and two grandchildren all came down one weekend to spruce up the house and fields for the reunion. They put a fresh coat of paint on the house, and bush-hogged the fields, while the grandchildren—ten-year-old Josh, and his ten-year-old cousin, Lizbeth—happily roamed the fields and woods, Just as their grandfather used to do as a boy.

"Things have been tough for Dad since Mom's passing. We feel that his spirit needs a lift. We're hoping that this reunion will help," Dan's daughter-in-law, Debbie, told me when she stopped at my place to invite me to the reunion and birthday party. Since I had been good friends with Dan and Anne, I was honored to be invited.

So, while the adults worked that weekend, Josh and his cousin Lizbeth, roamed the hills and hollows, collected neat-shaped rocks, and talked about what to give their Gramps for his birthday. Josh wanted his gift to be really special. Something that would truly lift his grandfather's spirit. But what would that be? He pondered and pondered.

A few days before the reunion, Josh and his mother drove to the Old Home Place again to finish last-minute preparations. But Josh was feeling desperate by this time, for he still didn't have a gift for Gramps, Debbie said. "I told Josh that we'd run to town in the morning, so he could look in the stores again. He'd better pick something out this time, the reunion is the day after tomorrow. But it seems he wants to give his grandfather something really special, not just any store-bought thing."

"That's so thoughtful of Josh," I said.

"Yes, except he's driving me batty. I told him to just draw him a picture or write him a poem, like Lizbeth is doing, but he didn't like that idea one bit."

Well, it seems that Josh was walking through the rolling, rocky field that afternoon when he felt something bumpy under his foot. He leaned down to examine his find since, to him, rocks were the jewels of the farm, and he lugged countless ones back to the city with him. But he was surprised that the bump under his foot wasn't a rock at all. No, it was something even better than a rock! Then, picking up his find, he raced across the field toward the house, whooping so loudly that countless birds, looking for newly hatched insects, flew off on startled wings.

"Mom! Mom! Come out and see what I found," Josh yelled at the top of his lungs, when he got closer. "I found the perfect gift for Gramps!"

When Debbie ran out and saw his find, she could hardly believe her eyes. "Why, Josh, you found Henry! Look you can still read the name

'Danny, 4/18/45' written on his back. There is no doubt that this is Henry, but I can't believe it's possible." She shook her head in amazement.

"Believe it, Mom. I have the proof right here in my hands," Josh told her. "And boy, will Gramps ever be surprised!"

Well, the birthday reunion was a great success. After a lot of eating and visiting, it was finally time for gifts. There were new shirts, new socks, a new robe and countless other gifts. Then Lizbeth recited her poem, and everyone gave her a standing ovation. Finally, Josh, came forward carrying a shoe box. I could hardly wait to see what was in it.

"Happy Birthday, Gramps," I heard him say loudly, handing over the box. "I didn't think this needed wrapping."

We all watched Dan lift the cover off the box and stare at the contents with an amazed expression. "It can't be," he finally muttered.

"But it is, Gramps," Josh said insistently. "It really is. See?"

Dan reached into the box and lifted out his gift gingerly.

"Look, everyone, Josh found my old box turtle, Henry. There is my name and the date I had found him, still on his back. Where did you ever find him, my boy?"

"In the field, Gramps, close to the creek."

"Pretty near where I had found him, back in 1945. Henry was a youngster back then, like myself. I carved my name in his shell." And as Dan was remembering, we noticed that his face had turned younger, and he looked almost boyish.

"I kept Henry for a couple of years, but then I released him back in the field. I even saw him a couple of times after that, but then I got older and all but forgot about Henry."

"You didn't forget, Gramps. You told me all about him, remember?" Josh said.

"Thank you, my boy, for this wonderful gift of a happy memory. It's the best gift I ever received," Dan finally said, wiping tears from his eyes. "I'm a blessed man, to have such a wonderful family." Then it was time to sing "Happy Birthday," while Henry enjoyed the piece of lettuce that Lizbeth put in the box for him.

Two days later, when it was time to go back to the city, Dan and Josh walked down to the creek together, to release Henry, once again. "I told Henry that we're both getting old now, but I think we may have a few good years left in us," Dan said when they came back to the house to get ready to leave.

"And who knows, we may meet again in the near future." Then he smiled and looked at his tow-headed grandson.

"They say turtles can live to be a hundred, you know," he said, ruffling Josh's hair.

"I know, Gramps," Josh replied, taking his grandfather's hand. "And if the good Lord be willing, so can grandfathers."

And as they got into their vehicles, to drive back to the city, I couldn't help but think that Anne was smiling down on them, from Heaven.

# That Day in the Bean Patch
## Tim Mills

*O*ur farm wasn't much to look at. When we first moved here in 1985 the land was cement-hard. Not one blade of grass. It had been used to raise horses, not grow crops. And the house was small and ugly. But my wife and I saw it for what it could be, not what it was. A home for us and our adopted daughter, Rebecca. We added another room and a bath, and painted the whole thing yellow. Did the work ourselves. Miss Bubbles— my wife's nickname—planted all kinds of flowers. The very next year, we had a garden.

Miss Bubbles was happy. At first. Back when we started dating as teenagers, she had a smile that would knock your socks off. But in time that smile faded. I tried not to notice because I had too much to do around the farm.

One fine summer day I was picking beans when Bubbles called out, "Tim! Come on up to the house and rest a bit with me." She was in the old, faded glider under the oak tree. She'd loved that spot ever since I'd put the swing up.

"Soon as I finish this row," I called back. But something drove me on to the next row and the next and then the one after that. A while later, I saw Bubbles get up from the swing and head inside, her shoulders slumped, dejected-like. *Strange how sitting in a swing could matter so much to a woma*n, I thought, then went back to bean picking.

One evening before supper Bubbles said to me, "Tim, take a look at this." I pulled my glasses out of my overalls pocket and took the piece of newspaper she handed me. She went right on talking while I read an ad about a mule for sale. "If you had a new mule you wouldn't have to work so hard. You're always saying that."

I took my glasses off and put them back into my pocket. "Bubbles, this looks like one fancy, expensive mule. Plus, he's a ways off. No sense driving all that way just to look at a mule we can't afford."

Her eyes narrowed. So did her mouth. Bubbles, Rebecca and I ate supper in silence, looking down at our food.

The next afternoon I was back out in the bean patch on my knees, picking in the hot Georgia sun. All at once some kind of strange hunger rose up in me. Not for food. I didn't know what to make of it. I reckon you'd call it a longing. A deep, gnawing misery, as if something had been chasing me for a long time and had finally caught up.

I thought about those days when Bubbles and I first started going together. We fell silly in love. We got married and adopted our Rebecca. Then one day, after twenty-two years, Bubbles announced, "Tim, this isn't much of a marriage. You're gone all week working, then you come home and work some more." I should have seen it coming. I was too busy working. But I always figured if a man worked hard, everything would turn out for good. Shows what I know. I told Bubbles I wanted to change. And I meant it. We moved here to Athens, Georgia, and started the farm. Slowly, though, I went back to my old ways. Now Bubbles was getting ready to call it quits again.

Suddenly, right there in the bean patch, I knew what it was I was hungry for. I started bawling. Me, a man who'd never cried, not even as a little fella, not even when we brought Rebecca home that first time. The sun was going down and a cool breeze picked up—a good time to pick beans. But I couldn't pick another one. Pretty soon my overalls were soaked with tears. I started calling to God, calling out loud. Then I heard my own name being called loud and clear. It wasn't Bubbles and it wasn't Rebecca and it wasn't any neighbors. The voice called my name again. Then a third time. I tried to crawl toward the voice, but I couldn't move. I fell over. Like I'd fainted or gone into a deep sleep. Felt like I was carried away. It wasn't scary; it was nice and restful.

I came to flat on my stomach in the bean patch, the rich smell of the dirt right in my face. I felt a peace and love more powerful than anything I'd ever felt before. I like to think I understand most things that happen in a garden, but I didn't understand this. Still don't. Though I did know who it was that called me that day in the bean patch.

I kept talking to God regularly. I told Him every thought I had and agreed with whatever it was he seemed to be saying. I figured as long as I was on my knees in the bean patch picking, I might as well use that time to listen. Listening is a kind of prayer too.

Not long after, I got a nudge to ask Bubbles, "You still got that newspaper clipping about that mule?"

She looked up. Her glasses were spattered with juice from the corn she was cutting off the cob, but I could still read her eyes. Like flashbulbs had gone off in them.

We went into the house, and I called the telephone number in the ad. Then we headed off to see this mule. Miss Bubbles seemed so happy riding along, you would have thought we were going to buy her a fine new dress or a dishwasher or something.

When we got to the place, there tied to a tree was the most beautiful mule I'd ever seen. A pretty red color. Looked smart too. Bubbles and I just sat in the car for a while with the motor turned off, looking out at the mule. He looked back at us. Sounds funny, but it was like love at first sight. I didn't want to break the mood, so I didn't mention anything about how much he was likely to cost.

We got out of the truck and walked over to the tree. I was rubbing the mule's nose when the owner came around the corner of the barn. Miss Bubbles was loving on the mule too.

"His name's Friday," the owner said. "Day he was born."

Everybody knows you don't give a work mule a name with two syllables, I thought. And I was right. This mule had never worked.

The price was much less than I'd feared. Maybe he'd lowered it some because he wanted the mule to have a good home and it was plain as day that Miss Bubbles and I already loved him. Bubbles opened her purse and I reached into my overalls pocket. We counted out our money. Would you believe that we had just what the man wanted? To the penny! He even agreed to deliver the mule for us.

"He has to have a new name," I said on the drive back home.

Bubbles sounded giddy. "Can I name him?" She gave it a lot of thought. It took her a while till one Sunday on our way to church she said, "I always loved Dr. Luke in the Bible. How about Luke for a name?"

He was stubborn, even ran away a few times. But as he settled down, he caught on pretty quickly. I think he liked his new name.

I still went out to the bean patch to talk and listen to God. It was there he told me about earthworms, how they can work for us. When we turn the ground with a plow, we interfere with that work. And when we kill them with chemicals, then we have to do all their work.

So I stopped using pesticides and I stopped plowing altogether. Instead, I used Luke to pull a tiller that broke up the ground just enough to help the earthworms get started. Wasn't long before I noticed a heap of worms.

The next thing God put into my head was the idea to build my own mill. Now my name might be Mills, but that didn't mean I knew anything about making my own mill. But I figured I'd at least give it a try.

Took some trial and error, but I ended up with a series of gears and shafts that turn when Luke, attached to a harness, walks his circles in the dirt. The mill can produce up to 100 pounds of corn meal or grits in an hour. One hundred pounds! I couldn't do that on my own if you gave me all week.

Bubbles and I sell our goods at the Daily Grocery Co-op and the Big City Farmer's Market in Athens. Our labels have a picture of Luke on them, and the names honor him too: Red Mule Grits, Red Mule Corn Meal, Red Mule Polenta, Red Mule English Porridge.

None of this would have happened without Bubbles. She found that ad, and God softened my heart, and we got Luke. I don't have to work as many hours these days. It means I can lay my bucket down in the bean patch and head for the house, where Miss Bubbles has fresh lemonade waiting. We settle down in the glider and swing back and forth, easylike.

# My Little Lamb

### Luanne Bandy Holzloehner

*I* pulled the barn door closed behind me, shutting out the bitter January cold and swirling snow. The ewe was on the floor of her stall, her head resting on a patch of straw. I stared at her swollen belly. *What a time to give birth*, I thought.

Her flanks heaved. Any time now. I saw the strain in her eyes and reached down to stroke her side. She snapped at my hand. I pulled back. What ever made Henry and me think we could raise sheep? I wondered. Or do any of this—build a log house, grow our own food, keep livestock for milk and eggs?

I was a city girl, but I'd always dreamed of moving to the country and living off the land. God's land. After my kids were grown, Henry and I got married—a second marriage for both—and we'd decided to start a second life too. We had given up the rat race, our daily commutes, our nine-to-five jobs. We had moved close to nature. We sold our city homes and bought five acres in Vermont dairy country. Our first night there I hugged Henry tightly and told him, "Our lives will be wonderful now."

We found a little white clapboard church that we liked, and dutifully introduced ourselves to our neighbors. I got a part-time job at a school and Henry took a job delivering newspapers, but mostly we stuck to ourselves and tried to make the farm work. Wasn't that the idea? To be far from civilization. To be independent. To live close to the land and the few sheep and cows we raised. Yet from the very beginning, it had been a struggle to survive. A lonely struggle.

I stared at the ewe, struggling herself now. *Lord, I thought this move would bring us closer to You. Why do You feel so far away?* I prayed.

I tossed a handful of fresh hay into the ewe's stall. It was all I could do for her right now. Then I stepped out the barn door, threw my weight against it to shut it and headed through the fierce wind to the house. I would check on her again after dinner.

Each day, it seemed, brought a new problem. One day our pickup rolled down the hill and plunged into the pond. Not long after, the tractor we used as a snowplow broke down and we had to fight a half-mile through ice and hip-deep snow just to reach the end of our driveway. Then our well ran dry. The workers kept drilling deeper and deeper into the ground looking for water, each foot costing precious dollars we didn't have.

Maybe this life was a terrible mistake, I thought, trudging through the snow. The work was endless. Maybe we should go back and live in the city again. At least that was something we knew. When something went wrong I could look in the yellow pages and make a call. Or if I ran out of something, I could knock on my next-door neighbor's door or run to the corner market. What were you supposed to do in the country at the end of a dirt road without a neighbor in sight?

Henry and I ate dinner in near silence. We did the dishes, then I pulled on Henry's heavy jacket and headed back to the barn. Inside, everything was still. My clouds of cold breath hung in the air. I peeked over the side of the stall. There, nestled in the matted hay, were two tiny balls of wool. Twins.

"You did it," I said to the ewe. I wanted to celebrate with her. But I saw in her eyes that something was wrong.

One of the babies was curled up, motionless, in the corner. Dead?

I bent over and picked it up. The lamb wriggled slightly in my arms. Relief washed over me. I carried it to its mother. "Help your baby," I urged her. But the ewe just pushed it aside. She had already given up on its survival. If the baby were to survive, it would be up to me.

One more hopeless thing, I thought. Still, how could I not try?

I tucked the tiny ball of fur beneath Henry's coat and carried her to our cabin. Henry quickly helped me arrange a little playpen with hay. Above it we placed a heat lamp to keep her warm. I decided to name her Lorrie.

For a week I looked after her constantly. Nights, I slept on an old recliner with the lamb snuggled in my lap and fed her every three hours with a baby bottle.

One night, as I cuddled her in my arms, she looked up at me with utter trust. That look unnerved me. *Who am I to save her?*, I thought. I could barely save myself.

*Please, Lord, save Lorrie*, I prayed. She's so weak and helpless. She needs you so much. And then more softly I added, So do I. I put her down on the floor. She stood for a moment on her wobbly legs. Then she sank weakly back to her knees.

I picked her up again and cuddled her in the chair. I started to doze off. A thought startled me awake. Take Lorrie to church tomorrow. I smiled, shook my head. *Crazy*, I thought to myself. *Take a lamb to church?* I shook my head again and went back to sleep.

The next morning I couldn't get the notion out of my head as I dressed for church. When I passed Lorrie on my way toward the door I grabbed her from her playpen. I wrapped her in a soft blue blanket and headed out to the pickup. Henry was waiting for me behind the wheel. He looked at me in disbelief.

"What are you doing with her?" he asked me.

"I'm bringing Lorrie with us," I told him quietly.

Henry started to protest, then just shook his head and helped us in.

We pulled up to the church and climbed out of the pickup truck. I took a deep breath, then walked to the entrance with Lorrie in my arms. The minister stood in the doorway, greeting parishioners.

"I'd like to say a few words after the service, if it's okay," I said to him.

He spotted the little lamb, curled up in the blanket. He raised his eyebrows, surprised, then nodded that it was okay.

I led Henry to a back pew. At the end of the service, I walked to the altar, hiding Lorrie from view. Then I turned to the congregation and unwrapped the blanket. People stared and murmured when they saw Lorrie.

I wasn't sure what I wanted to say. But deep inside I knew I had to do this. I set Lorrie down on her wobbly limbs. As she struggled to walk, I explained how important it had become for me that she survive. And then the words just spilled out.

"I thought life would be easy here, that I could make it on my own. But I am weak and helpless. Sometimes I feel like there isn't any help. Then I try to remember, 'The Lord is my shepherd and I shall not want...'" My voice trailed off. Henry stood at the back of the church, his cap in his hand, blinking back tears.

Silence.

I picked Lorrie up, lowered my head to hide my face and headed quickly toward the door. But before I could reach it the congregation was on their feet, closing in around me.

A little girl's hand reached out to pet Lorrie. A woman's arm tightened around my shoulders. Then another and another until it felt like the whole church was holding me, holding me the way I held that little lamb, the way the Lord would always hold me closer and closer.

At last I had found what I had been seeking all along.

# Our Hero, Hurricane

## Toni Drugmand

$\mathcal{Y}$ou couldn't sit by watching the television images from New Orleans and elsewhere in the aftermath of Hurricane Katrina and not be affected. Thousands of people left homeless, families torn asunder, desperate people forced to leave their pets behind.

As a professional dog trainer I was a member of an Internet mailing list for trainers who specialized in problem dogs. June Towler sent out a plea for help. She was part of a group called Stealth Volunteers.

Working in teams, the "Stealths" paddled through a still-flooded New Orleans that was eerily quiet. They battled unsafe waters, treacherous debris and stifling summer humidity searching for animals too weak to meow or cry. The rescued animals went to the Lamar Dixon Equestrian Center outside of New Orleans, or to Humane Society shelters all over the country.

June Towler described one dog, a pit bull, who was in a Santa Fe, New Mexico, shelter. "He is about eighteen months old and only weighs thirty-eight pounds," June wrote. "He has been labeled unadoptable and vicious, and is scheduled to be euthanized. I believe that if given a chance he may not be vicious at all."

It wasn't hard for me to imagine the dog's situation. Already traumatized by the hurricane, he was now cooped up inside a cage in a crowded shelter. He deserved a chance. I e-mailed June back: "I'm in Phoenix," I wrote, "but I'm willing at least to evaluate him. Somehow."

Now, how to get him? I called my old friend Storm, a Special Forces soldier who had experience with dogs. He happened to love pit bulls and was glad to help out "a survivor." Storm agreed to pick up the dog and bring him the five hundred miles to me.

On New Year's Eve, Storm's pickup rolled into my driveway. Storm opened the door and out came one wild dog. He pulled on the leash, jumped up and sniffed everything in sight. Storm could barely hold him back. He brought him into the house and let him go. The dog barreled around through every room like a hurricane on four legs blowing through the house.

"Hurricane!" Storm said. "That's what you should name him!"

We got Hurricane into a dog crate, and Storm told me about the trip. "At first he was jumping around in the truck, looking at everything. But after a while he lay down up front so he could see my face."

"So you think he's got potential?" I said. "You think he could be trained?"

"I've never seen a dog as alert as this one," Storm said. "He'd be sleeping in the back of the truck, and if I so much as turned my head to look at him he woke up. If I got out to get food or fuel up he'd watch for me. When I came back he'd kiss me hello and hop into the back again. To be honest, I wish I could keep this dog myself."

*Bang!* Hurricane hurled himself against the door to his crate. It flew open and he tumbled out, grinning at us, his tongue hanging out to one side.

"We'd better get to work," I said.

"Yeah," said Storm. "He's a lot like an unguided missile—friendly, but totally undisciplined."

Once I got Hurricane's attention his progress was amazing. Everyone on my staff wanted a turn with him. After only ten days he could heel, sit, run to his place and stay—all off leash! Hurricane would be a great addition to any family who adopted him.

It looked like Hurricane had gotten his happy ending after all. But his story wasn't over yet. I got a call from Lisa Harford, a dog trainer in New Jersey. Lisa was part of the FEMA search-and-rescue team.

"We're looking for a dog," she said, "a healthy, energetic, nonaggressive dog who can cope with the stress of being around other dogs and handlers and rescue workers in the confusion of a rescue site."

Could this be the right place for Hurricane? Could a rescued dog become a rescuer? Hurricane certainly learned quickly and loved people— he even climbed like a mountain goat.

"I've got just the dog for you," I told her. Even though it meant Storm and I had to say good-bye to him.

Hurricane has taken to Lisa and her FEMA team and will be in training in New Jersey for six months or so before going on active duty. "I don't have any major doubts about his passing the final tests," Lisa said last time we spoke, "but if he doesn't, I can assure you Hurricane will never be homeless again."

Before Hurricane left on his latest adventure, Storm got down on his knees and gave him a big hug. "Remember, son," Storm whispered in Hurricane's flopped ear, "when all the angels are busy, God sends a dog."

That's Hurricane, all right. Our angel-in-training. Our hero.

# Roadblock

## Celin Wood

*M*orning sun shone through the windshield, but the little country road I took to work each day had lost its charm. It wasn't the scenery, or the road itself. It was the job I hated at the end of it. Personnel had changed with a local election. So did the atmosphere in the office, and not for the better. The stress was killing me.

I steered my van into a parking space. *Lord, I can't keep on like this*, I thought as I walked inside. Surely God had heard my pleas for help. Was I missing His answer? *Could You give me a sign I'm sure to understand?* I asked Him.

I settled in at my desk. Mary called to see how I was doing. We'd been friends for years. When management changed I'd confided my fears to her. She encouraged me as I tried to adjust to the new situation. When I confessed things weren't getting any better, Mary had supported me in trying to grin and bear it. In fact, she gave me the resin eagle that sat front and center on my desk. It was supposed to remind me to fly above the minutia and soar. I glanced at the eagle now. "You know, Mary," I said, "it's really hard to fly with the eagles when you're surrounded by turkeys!"

Mary laughed. "You should quit."

"If I were offered another job I'd take it in a second," I said. "But what if I left this job and couldn't get another? At least now I have security."

Security. That was the one good thing about my job. I tried to remember it the rest of the day, as I counted the minutes until I could leave. Mary's words kept running through my mind. Maybe you should quit. It was so tempting.

But the next morning I was back in my van, heading down the country road as always. There was something up ahead. I slowed. An animal or bird was blocking the road—a whole group of something. I crept closer. Huge birds came into focus. Turkeys. Big, glossy, brown-black turkeys.

I'd never seen a turkey up close. Now they were all around me. I started to laugh and cry all at once. I had asked God for a sign I couldn't miss, and He had surrounded me with turkeys—literally!

I turned around and called in—to announce my resignation. I had been waiting for another job to come to me before I could leave. Now I knew I could fly without one. I had skills, I had determination, and a little bit of savings to tide me over till I found a new job. Which I did. Nowadays I may soar with the eagles, but turkeys will always hold a special place in my heart.

# Sit. Stay. Pray.

*Rachel Bickford*

*S*unday afternoon, five o'clock sharp. The organ hums while I set re-
freshments on the front table and walk to the pulpit. I'm the pastor of
Pilgrim Congregational Church in North Weymouth, Massachusetts,
and my parishioners are my second family. I look out at my regulars.
There's Lucy, an older gal with a spring in her step and perfectly coiffed
blonde curls. Sam, in his usual seat in the front pew, gazes back at me
with his soulful brown eyes. Chloe, a rambunctious youngster, fidgets a
little, but she'll settle down when the choir begins. Oh, there's something
I should mention. Lucy is a terrier, Sam is a pug and Chloe is a Bernese
mountain dog.

Our service for people and their pets started last October. Sometimes, though, I wonder if the seed wasn't planted earlier. Growing up,
I'd wanted to be a vet, but in my twenties I felt called to seminary. After
seven years at Pilgrim Congregational, I still loved coming to work. But
folks just weren't coming to church as much anymore. Too many sport-
ing events on Sundays and too little faith. I looked out at the half-empty
sanctuary one Sunday and thought, *Lord, what can I do to get people as
excited as I am about coming to church?*

A few days later, I got an e-mail from an old friend who needed some
extra prayers. I bowed my head. That's when my gaze fell on my two

apricot cockapoos, Tugger and Indy, curled up at my feet. One of my favorite verses, Psalm 148, suddenly came to mind: Let all wild animals and small creatures and flying birds praise the Lord. All animals praise the Lord.

Something about those words gave me a charge. Plenty of people loved bringing their dogs to our town dog park. What if those folks could bring their dogs to church?

"Honey, I have an idea," I said to my husband, Peter, that evening. "People should be able to bring their dogs to church. Dogs give unconditional love and support. I mean, it just makes sense...or does it?"

"Bring...their dogs...to church," he said slowly, then paused. "Actually, Rachel, that's so wild, it just might work."

That week I mentioned the idea to my fellow pastors, hoping they wouldn't think I'd lost it. They didn't. They loved it! We advertised a Sunday afternoon service. It would be like our more formal one, but after worship we'd serve biscuits and toss tennis balls with our dogs in the side yard. All breeds, as long as they were leashed, were welcome. We decided on a name: Woof 'n' Worship.

That first Sunday I was nervous. Maybe I hadn't thought things through. What if the dogs didn't get along? *Lord, is this too crazy?*, I wondered, walking Tugger and Indy to the pulpit with me. I looked up. The sea of furry faces, and the smiling people in the pews beside them, made me smile too. Before long we had 150 people—150! The dogs got along famously. I giggled when, during my first reading, a handsome German shepherd with a clownish grin licked a tiny Chihuahua's ears. Later, the choir sang "Amazing Grace." Everyone roared when Pee Wee, a schnauzer, began howling along. He was almost in key! The best perk of all is that people are reaching out to each other more. The dogs are a great icebreaker. "Sometimes I feel out of place among all the families here," a single college student told me. "But with Chewy, I fit right in." One woman who's battling breast cancer confided, "Whenever I'm tempted to stay in bed, I remember my responsibility to Diego. We've made so many new friends from bringing him to church."

I peer out from my pulpit and take another look at my regulars. Yup, it's true, my church is going to the dogs—and that's just fine with me. Sometimes, when we ask God for a solution to a problem, His answer is far better (and crazier!) than we could ever imagine on our own.

# Living Together

Hurt no living thing;
 Ladybird, nor butterfly,
Nor moth with dusty wing,
 Nor cricket chirping cheerily;
Nor grasshopper so light of leap.
 Nor dancing gnat, nor beetle fat,
Nor harmless worms that creep.

—CHRISTINA ROSSETTI

# Leap of Love
## Summer Sheldon

_I_t should have been the perfect date for Ryan and me—a late summer hike through majestic Silver Falls State Park, the largest in Oregon. The scene around us was out of a nature film: a thick forest of dark, moss-covered evergreens, dewy, drooping ferns and fluorescent clovers lining the trail. We strolled alongside a gurgling creek, walking my brother's dog, Little Pig, who stopped now and again to sniff a random flower or patch of grass. A romantic, serene moment. Except Ryan just had to bring up what was bothering him. What was bothering me too. "All I'm saying is it doesn't feel like you're that into me sometimes," Ryan said.

I sighed. "Can we change the subject?"

Ryan just stared at the ground. Little Pig caught up to us and rubbed up against Ryan's leg. It was surprising how well he'd taken to Ryan, showering him with affection. I, on the other hand, couldn't be so bold. I did love Ryan—but I hadn't been able to show it. Commitment. The word scared me. I didn't think I could commit to anyone. Was it unfair to lead Ryan on? Walking that trail, I felt like we were headed toward a breakup. I pulled a couple paces ahead. It had been the same story since I was sixteen. That was when my parents announced they were going to take a three-month "trial separation." I'd thought my parents had a good marriage and loved each other, but within two weeks they both had lawyers and couldn't have a conversation that didn't become a screaming match. They attacked one another and accused me of taking sides. If I couldn't trust my parents' love, then whose love could I trust? The one thing I hung on to was my trust in God. Of that I was pretty certain. But to take that leap and trust another human being with my deepest desires frightened me. Every time I got close to a guy, I pulled away.

Even sweet Ryan. When I met him in college, I took it slow. I came up with different degrees of relationships—"serious friending" came before "casual dating," which progressed into "serious dating"—before I was willing to be called his girlfriend. Ryan put up with my silliness over the past two years, but I knew it was hard for him whenever he said he loved me and I couldn't say it back. A walk through the park with Little Pig could lighten the mood, I thought. But now I'd hurt Ryan again. *God*, I prayed silently, *help me not feel this fear. Help me learn how to love him. To trust.* Silently, Ryan and I followed the trail as it dipped beneath the thirty-foot-high bridge for the Silver Falls Highway that cuts through the park. We came out on the other side and I looked back for Little Pig. The trail was empty. "Did you see where he went?" I asked. Ryan shook his head.

"Little Pig!" he called. I echoed him. But Little Pig didn't come running.

"Maybe he chased a squirrel or something," Ryan said. "Don't worry, we'll find him."

*He's never run off before*, I thought. I wouldn't have been surprised six months earlier, when my brother first found him. Back then, Little Pig was a half-starved blue heeler, with a torn ear and an eye patch marking, that my brother found abandoned in a grocery store parking lot. He wasn't that well behaved at the time. He backed away from strangers and didn't always obey. He'd clearly been abused. The sight of someone using a broom would set him off barking. But slowly Little Pig's behavior improved as he learned to trust the people in his life. I couldn't imagine him not responding to his name.

"Little Pig!" I shouted again, jogging up the trail. I stepped off the trail into the bushes. "Little Pig!" No answer. Could he have gotten lost? Did he fall into the creek? I couldn't bear to think about it. He was my brother's dog, but he felt like mine too.

I was the one who gave him his name. One day I was playing with him outside, laughing as he rolled around in the dirt. "You're as happy as a little pig!" I said. The name stuck.

This summer I worked at the same job as my brother and hung out with Little Pig every day. We became pals—I'd feed him some of my sandwich at lunch; he'd rest his head in my lap. What if we don't find him? Tears started to pool in my eyes. Ryan put his arm around me. "Don't cry, Summer. You know what? He's probably looking for us." I looked at Ryan. Something about his voice, his smile, the way he held me was so reassuring. I could feel that flutter in my heart, telling me Ryan was the one—but like all those other times, I was still too afraid to say a thing. "Let's go back to the bridge," Ryan said. "He's probably there waiting." We walked back under the bridge. We both heard it at the same time. Is that a whine? Where is it coming from? Just then a loud screech came from the bridge above. A car swerving. I looked up. Oh no! There was Little Pig, his gray nose sticking through the guardrail. He must've gone up the steep embankment when we went down and couldn't figure out how to get back. I called to him, "Little Pig!"

He perked up immediately, turned his head and looked straight down at me and Ryan, standing on the trail thirty feet below. Then he took a step back from the rail, paused for a second and dashed forward. What is he . . . .? Before I could tell him to stay, he sprung off his hind legs and hurled his forty-pound body up into the air—over the rail. I couldn't breathe. I watched helplessly as he plummeted toward the creek below. He hit the water with a splash. Ryan and I raced into the water after him.

I pictured myself carrying his shattered body back to the car. Were there any vets nearby? How could I've been so stupid as to let him off his leash?

Suddenly, Little Pig's head popped up in the water. His paws paddled wildly toward us, his pink tongue hanging out—and what looked for all the world like a goofy smile on his face. Ryan reached out and grabbed him. The second we climbed out onto the bank, Little Pig jumped on me, licking my face, relieved to have found us. I laughed in disbelief. "Sit! I need to check if anything's broken!" I demanded. But he was so happy, he wouldn't stop bouncing around. "He seems fine to me," Ryan said. "It's a miracle." No doubt it was.

Only God could've guided Little Pig's path. Ryan helped me up, and we walked back to the car, keeping a close eye on Little Pig. I couldn't stop thinking about what that crazy dog had done. A dog that had suffered terrible unkindness made a fearless leap. Fearless because he trusted. Trust cancels fear. Was that the lesson, the answer to my prayer? I stopped walking and put my arms around Ryan. Maybe it was time to take a leap of my own.

# Samuel Emmanuel

### Sue Kjellsen

*N*ot everyone loves cats, but then again the orange tabby wasn't your usual stray. He was healthy and well fed (okay, maybe even a bit plump). He'd been hanging around outside Emmanuel Episcopal Church for days, and I just knew he was lost. I brought him some food my own cats "decided" to donate and set it outside next to a bowl of water. He made a beeline for it and tucked right in, eating as if he'd never seen food before. *Poor thing*, I thought. *What are we going to do with you?* We had a big enough job reaching out to people in our community.

I watched the classifieds, searching for a "lost cat" ad. But none appeared. It looked like this cat needed a home and the church looked like the right place for him.

For some reason he seemed like a "Sam" to me. At least that's how I introduced him to our sexton, Van Womble. "I can't keep a pet in my apartment," he said. "But if Sam wants to hang around here, I'll help you look after him." Our deacon, Tally Bandy, was another cat lover and she willingly pitched in to help care for Sam. She couldn't have cats at home either, so to her he was sent to fill that "cat place" in her heart.

But what would my boss, the rector, Hank Franklin, have to say about a church cat? Hank didn't like cats and complained about the two he had at home. But Sam must have grown on him, because one day he announced, "That cat should have a proper name. From now on, he's 'Samuel Emmanuel.'" And so Samuel Emmanuel became a member of our church.

One Sunday, right in the middle of the service, Sam made a grand entrance, marching down the center aisle with his tail straight up in the air. Hank never missed a beat. "Good morning, Samuel," he said and then went right on with his sermon.

Sam became a regular, always able to find a willing lap in the congregation. He'd curl up there until the sermon was over then, newly edified, jump down and leave. In time, his "ministry" expanded. Our students mobbed him whenever they saw him. Our first-grade class even wrote and illustrated a book about Sam. But who loved him most of all? You guessed it, Hank. People outside the church loved Sam too. I got to talking to a woman at the supermarket once and was puzzled when she asked how Sam was doing. She didn't go to our church. "How on earth do you know Sam?" I asked. "Oh, I attend a meeting there and Sam always comes too." I realized she must attend one of the AA groups that meet at our church. I could picture her holding Sam on her lap, comforted while she stroked his fur, and talking about the difficult things in her life.

Sam became our ambassador of goodwill. He greeted the families who strolled through our neighborhood and inspected the cars parked in front of the church to make sure they belonged. He attended some weddings and most funerals. Except one.

A sudden heart attack took Hank from us. We were devastated. In all of the commotion of the funeral, Sam was nowhere to be found. After everyone left, Van spotted Sam lying on the mound of dirt where Hank's ashes had been buried. And there Sam stayed for two days. I like to think our ambassador of goodwill was saying good-bye to his friend.

Now, Sam greets all of us as we arrive for work. After he's had his breakfast, he takes his place under a bench not far from Hank. When I catch sight of Sam lying there, I think of words from our prayer book: "Keep watch, dear Lord, with those who work, or watch, or weep . . . and give your angels charge over those who sleep." A stray? No, Samuel Emmanuel was definitely sent.

# A Home for Gus

*Crystal Ward Kent*

$T$he first four to five years of Gus's life are a mystery. The little Jack Russell terrier had lived on a farm for a time, and then was given to another family. They had him for only a year, then decided he was too wild. Gus's next stop was the animal shelter. It would either mean the start of a new life—and a real home—or it would be his final stop.

Gus was cute and perky, and shelter staff thought he could be easily placed. They featured his photo in a mailing, and soon visitors began seeking him out for adoption. A family with small children decided to take him home. They wanted a small dog, and the children thought he looked like "Wishbone," a popular children's TV character.

Unfortunately, the adoption was a disaster. Within two months, Gus was back at the shelter. The family complained that the dog was difficult to handle, aggressive, and could only be walked on a chain leash. He urinated in his bed and was too rambunctious, in short, Gus was not a suitable pet.

Back at the shelter, Gus began to wreak more havoc. Some volunteers did not want to walk him—he pulled aggressively on his leash, and growled fiercely as he wrestled with his nylon enemy. When the door to his pen was opened, he darted out, instigating a daily game of catch-me-if-you-can. He was very vocal, barking constantly, and some personnel were intimidated by his noise. He was untrained and seemed untrainable.

Things were looking dark indeed, when Gus's guardian angel appeared, in the form of a new staffer named Jennifer. Jennifer was a dog trainer with experience with Jack Russell terriers; she had owned Jack Russells in the past, and had one now. The shelter manager asked her to evaluate Gus. Could this little dog become a good companion?

When Jennifer first saw Gus he was bouncing six feet straight up in the air, and the walls reverberated with his barking.

"I could hear him long before I saw him," she recalls. "Oh, he had a lot to say! When I got closer, I could see this little ball of brown and white fur hurling itself up and down, like it was on springs. I knew that Gus and I were about to have an interesting relationship."

Jennifer knew that much of Gus's problem stemmed from the fact that his previous owners had little knowledge of Jack Russell terriers. Jack Russells are strong-willed, smart and tenacious—like all terriers. They have a strong prey drive, like to run and need to burn off plenty of energy. They can be hyper and vocal, and do best if they have some kind of job, or other way to occupy their time.

Gus, like others of his breed, was small—about twenty pounds and fifteen inches tall—but he was all muscle. Despite his size, he was quite capable of being more than a handful on a leash.

Jennifer realized that Gus's problem was two-fold. First, no one had taken the time to train him. Second, because he was difficult, he often didn't get walked or played with, that left him with energy to burn and made him frustrated. The whole situation was a vicious circle—which she must break. Jennifer knew that if she failed, Gus's chance for a happy home was probably gone. He was six-years-old. He had three homes and been returned to the shelter once already. Younger, calmer dogs would be chosen before him, and his track record would put people off.

But Jennifer believed that somewhere inside Gus was a wonderful companion waiting to be discovered. She went to work.

First, Jennifer tested Gus for aggression. She was surprised to find that the "wild dog" was actually very gentle and easily let Jennifer pet him over his whole body. In fact, he lay down, rolled over and looked away—a canine sign of submission. As she spent time with him, she discovered that if anything, Gus was defensive-aggressive. He often pretended aggression because he was scared. He figured that if he acted fierce, that would scare off any threat and he wouldn't be hurt. Jennifer became convinced that somewhere in Gus's puppyhood, he had been badly frightened and possibly abused. He had never truly bonded with anyone. No one had loved him enough to win his trust.

Gus's urination problem also stemmed from fear. He urinated slightly when excited or frightened. If he could be given sense of security, the urinating would stop.

Like many terriers, Gus was very intelligent, and full of play. He loved games and needed them to channel his abundant energy and challenge his active mind. Using a healthy mix of play and work, Jennifer quickly taught him basic commands. The little dog thrived on learning and quickly proved he was trainable. The leash problem was also resolved—if Jennifer ignored Gus's frantic tugging on the leash, he got bored and stopped. When his previous handlers had tugged back, trying to dominate Gus over the leash, the dog thought it was a tug-of-war game and responded with wile enthusiasm.

Gus's intelligence showed itself in his vocalizations. He had an extensive range of growls and barks, and much of his talk was just that—dog talk. He was not behaving fiercely, just communicating his many opinions the only way he knew how. As Gus began to have more play and activity, and a more structured day, his random, frantic barking lessened.

Jennifer decided Gus was ready for the final test—time in a home. She proposed having him spend a week with her. The shelter manager readily agreed, but there were some hurdles.

Jennifer already had a female Jack Russell Terrier at home. The aptly named Diva believed she ruled the roost, and so far, had never allowed any other dog to set foot on her turf, much less live there for a week. Jennifer decided to introduce the two dogs at the shelter, on neutral ground. If all went well, Gus would visit.

Amazingly, Diva and Gus hit it off, and Diva "consented" for Gus to come to her home. As the trio left, shelter staff winked at each other. They wondered if Gus would be back.

As the week passed, Jennifer was amazed at how well Gus fit in. He and Diva played non-stop; they shared toys and even Diva's dog bed. Gus was on his best behavior and obeyed commands to stay off furniture. There were no urination incidents. He was a wonderful companion.

Jennifer knew she didn't want to let Gus go. He was ready for adoption, but something had happened during their long work sessions together. He had become a friend. She loved the feisty little dog, and looking at him curled happily with Diva, she thought "this is his family."

There was one problem. Jennifer was getting married in one week. When she broached possibly keeping Gus to her fiancé, he was adamant. No more dogs! Diva was enough.

"Dmitri said he was concerned about the upkeep of two dogs, the hair and all of that," recalls Jennifer. "But mostly, he felt left out. Diva was my dog—that was plain. Dmitri felt that Gus would be my dog, too, and he wanted his own dog, that he picked out. He never said any of this, but I sensed it—and evidently, Gus sensed it too."

Jennifer finally coaxed Dmitri into at least meeting Gus and seeing how far he had come. The minute Dmitri sat down in the living room chair, Gus leaped into his lap, curled up and went to sleep. Dmitri was won over instantly. This was his dog after all!

The shelter staff were not surprised to hear that Jennifer wanted to adopt Gus. They happily presented him to her and Dmitri as a wedding present, knowing that the tough little terrier would live happily ever after in this home.

"He is so much a part of our family," says Jennifer. "He has his own toy box, and he and Diva are best buddies. He follows her lead on everything—good habits and bad, I'm afraid. And he is truly bonded now—for the first time in his life he has a family to love. He can't wait for my husband to get home. First thing, he's up in his lap wanting to be hugged. This was truly a match made in heaven."

# Love Bird
### Linda Wagner

*A*nimals were always welcome in my house. So when a little girl in my son Eric's kindergarten class found a cracked bird's egg on the ground, she brought it right to our front door. "Can you take care of it, Mrs. Wagner?" she asked, offering up the challenge in her palms.

The egg was hatching right before my eyes. A tiny beak pecked out through the shell. "I'll do my best," I promised, and took the lost little creature in. I found a plastic dish and put the egg inside. Peck by peck a wet brown chick fought its way out. She was no bigger than a nickel.

My husband, Dan, watched over my shoulder. "Tiny little squirt, isn't she?" he said.

"She sure is. I think that's what I'll call her. Squirt."

I hunted down an eyedropper just small enough to fit in her beak. The pet shop didn't carry baby bird food, but the salesman thought kitten formula might do the trick. Squirt seemed to like it. We set her up in a cage with newspaper lining. Every day I drove home from work on my lunch hour to feed her.

One afternoon my son Jason watched me give Squirt her daily bath. Her happy chirps made me believe this was the high point of her day. I splashed water with my fingers in a saucer. Squirt fluttered her wings beside them.

"I hope she stays right here with us forever," said Jason.

"Squirt's going back to the wild as soon as she's ready," I explained. "That's where she belongs. God wants us to love all His animals just the way He made them."

I didn't tell Jason that I wasn't looking forward to losing her either. Squirt was like no wild bird I'd ever seen. She rode around on my shoulder, sang duets with me as I did laundry. At dawn she hopped onto my pillow and sang when I opened my eyes. In the evening, Squirt flew into a wicker basket hanging on the living room wall. She'd made a nest inside it and didn't ever come out after sundown. Nobody had to teach Squirt that flying around the house in the dark was dangerous. Instinct took care of that.

Dan chuckled one night watching me give her a gentle good-night kiss on her beak, even though Squirt didn't know what it meant. "Now the baby's all tucked in," he said.

I laughed. "Don't worry. I'm not getting any ideas about putting any babies to bed. Our family of four is enough."

But not long after Dan and I got a big surprise: I was pregnant! Planned or not, I was overjoyed by the news. Squirt watched with great interest as I sorted through old infant clothes and furniture, preparing for the exciting new arrival.

Six weeks into my pregnancy, I started spotting. We took the boys to a neighbor's, and Dan drove me to the emergency room. "There's really nothing we can do this early," the doctor told us. "Just go home and try to get some rest."

It was late when we got home. I checked on Squirt. She was sound asleep in her nest. I climbed into bed. The bleeding only got worse.

Dan called the doctor. I wasn't going to have a baby after all.

"Ask him if we can see him in the morning," I said. "I can't face another hospital trip."

The doctor told Dan to try and keep me comfortable. He hovered around me, wanting so much to help. But Dan could not do any more than the doctor could. A part of me had died. I lay in bed with a cold, empty place inside me. A place meant for my baby. Not even my husband's love could reach it. *God, please let me feel Your love.*

Something rustled on my pillow. Squirt? Not at this hour. No way could she fly to me through the dark house. But when I looked there she was, right on my pillow. She leaned forward and touched her beak to my lips.

"Dan," I whispered, "Squirt just gave me the sweetest kiss."

Warmth flooded all through me, straight to that cold place I'd thought was chilled forever. God had found a way to reach me: with an impossible kiss that only His love could make possible.

It took a while, but eventually Dan and the boys and I got used to our little family of four again. And Squirt was always there to lift my spirits on the bad days.

After five years with us, something must have told Squirt she was ready. A flock of birds flew overhead one day and Squirt joined them. I waved good-bye from the front porch as Squirt soared across the blue sky like a promise. Where she flies, God's love goes with her. There's no place on earth it can't reach.

# Ditto, Darling

*Ginny Greene*

$\mathcal{G}$retchen circled twice and then flopped on the floor at my side of the bed. A sigh three times bigger than her boxer body vented all her stored-up tension. Sometime I early puppyhood, our family pet had made it her life's purpose to see her people settled into bed at the end of the day.

Not that she didn't have many other things to do. A credit to her ancestors, which had been selectively bred from early eighteenth-century Germany, Gretchen was built like a coiled spring. Pushed to describe her in one word, I would have to say "effervescent." Brave and loyal, she was made for fun and play. An ambitious daily schedule kept her on the run all day long. Before the final farewell of the setting sun, she would dash across the fields, visit with neighbors, bully birds at the stream, chase cows and dodge squealing granddaughters whirling on the tire swing.

After sundown, the urgings of her own dreamland were barred by the fact that all her humans were still awake. Gretchen nudged us off to bed, one at a time. We were slow to realize the concentrated effort she put into herding us to the Land of Nod each and every evening. That loud sigh voiced her thoughts: *Phew! Finally! What a day!* Then she was off to chase wild rabbits and to howl with phantom wolves in her dreams.

Near the end of Gretchen's puppyhood, we relocated. She helped, bounding from van to house and room to room, her face alive with discovery and infectious joy. The house, set in Washington state's gorgeous orchard country, had a pull-down ladder stairway to the bedroom upstairs. Karen, our youngest, claimed dibs on the roomy attic. A string of helpers carried her belongings up the vertical staircase, organizing a choreographed group effort to get her bed and furnishings up there. Truth be told, it took a group effort to get me up there, vertigo intact. While we off-loaded furniture and boxes and bedsprings, Gretchen's fun ended at the bottom of the stairs each time we ascended into the great gaping maw.

Hubby thought it would be neat if Gretchen would climb the ladder, so he coaxed her with a bite of his banana, unsure whether the fruit would entice her. He actually thought it might take days and days and expensive steak bits to train her, but she whimpered twice and was up the stairs to nab the prize. It surprised her as much as us, especially when she turned around and looked back down. (But that's another banana.)

We taught our pet to speak too. All it took was praise and treats for every accidental noise that resembled dog talk. She spoke on request, as long as she sniffed a dog biscuit tucked in our hand. Pretty soon she assembled sounds in a string of dog language. It seemed natural for us to respond. It led to pleasant conversations, full of lively dialogue.

Oh, how I wish it were as easy training kids. Our daughter Karen, who was approaching the fringes of adulthood, stretched the boundary of our home rules to elastic fatigue on a daily basis. She worked in town, and we lived up a twisty mountain road, and it was winter. Fretting traced lines across my brow every evening from quitting time until she walked in our door. If she went out with friends afterward and didn't call me—and she often didn't—my fears spiraled up the worry scale. Driving on packed snow in sub-zero temperatures rated a certain level of worry, but worse was the thought of her behind the wheel during a "heat wave" thaw at thirty-two degrees, which created the slipperiest ice of all.

I always knew when Karen got home by our puppy's stand-issue spirited "Welcome home!" Late or not, Gretchen was always glad to see her favorite human come through the door.

Then came the night when my daughter was later than ever before. Worry escalated to near anguish. I sat up waiting, a knot in my stomach, and read (sort of) and then watched television (not really). One of my envisioned worst-case scenarios saw Karen stuck in the snow; another saw her dangling over the edge somewhere along the twenty-minute drive up our mountain road. Logic insisted that since I hadn't heard from any downhill neighbors, she probably wasn't stuck. The tire in the heater stove died to coals; the chill finally sent me to bed. Gretchen stationed herself in the doorway, her sigh still pent up inside.

It was way past two o'clock in the morning when I heard the front door close ever so gently. Gretchen came uncoiled. She unleashed her wrath in a tirade of doggy whimpers, wa-yaws and woo-hoos. She scolded Karen for worrying us, for endangering herself, for being out far too late. And furthermore, Karen should not have been out so late on a week night, no matter how grown-up she was getting!

My errant daughter tried to shush Gretchen, but the scolding didn't stop. Gretchen's doggy harangue sounded eerily English: "Where have you been? I've been worried sick!"

I listened from the bedroom, snuggled deep in blankets. Hubby tapped my arm, and we grinned at each other like conspirators.

Gretchen dogged Karen's every step across the dark room. The verbal lashing included every word we'd taught her and a few more besides! Karen had never quite seen her unacceptable behavior in such a light.

There was no doubt she'd exceeded the limits, not only in my eyes, but also in Gretchen's.

Karen headed for her stairs. By then, she was past the embarrassment of getting caught and was laughing with disbelief at the comic aspect of the scene. It got worse.

She stepped up the first two stairs. Gretchen leaped around her and beat her to the top. From the landing the dog loomed over her like an angry mom with arms akimbo and an accusing glare. Gretchen was "in her face" all the way up the stairs.

"Okay! Okay!" Karen begged, finally contrite.

Gretchen's discipline was so effective, I didn't even need to get out of bed. From deep in my warm winter blankets, I lifted my head an inch off the pillow and hollered through the cold night air "Ditto, darling!"

# Squirrels!

*Jane Kise*

I'd barely walked through the front door that December evening, and already my brain was abuzz with everything that needed to get done before I turned in. Look over the kids' homework while my husband, Brian, worked on a paper for his class the next night. Help eleven-year-old Mari pick out her clothes for tomorrow. Make sure Dan, thirteen, had his music books packed for his piano lessons. Get a jump on cleaning the house, since the relatives—all twenty-two of them—would be coming for Christmas. Do my own graduate school homework. All this in the few short hours between wolfing down dinner and collapsing into bed.

At least dinner was taken care of. I'd left meatloaf and potatoes in the fridge, with baking instructions. Strange, I couldn't smell anything cooking. I walked into the kitchen. It was dark.

"Brian?" I called, flipping on the light. No response. I heard voices coming from the backyard. I opened the sliding door and stuck my head out. In the dim light I could see Brian, Dan and Mari in the middle of our yard huddled under the pole the old box bird feeder sat on. Or the squirrel feeder, as the kids had taken to calling it, because of the constant onslaughts from ravenous squirrels.

"What are you guys doing out there?" I called. The three of them were fiddling around with what looked like a length of clothesline and some poles from our volleyball set with a bunch of crazy stuff hanging from it. "Why didn't you start cooking dinner?"

"Dinner had to wait, Honey," Brian yelled back. "We're building a squirrel obstacle course."

"A what?"

"Isn't that a great idea?" Dan shouted. "Dad said we were never going to keep the squirrels out of the bird feeder, so we should at least make it challenging for them to get to it."

With everything on our to-do list, they were worried about squirrels? I jerked the sliding door shut. Unbelievable. But that was my husband, being "creative" again. I threw the meatloaf and potatoes into the oven. They should've known better. Especially Brian. When he and the kids piled into the kitchen twenty minutes later, I let them know it.

"I don't suppose you've gotten started on your homework," I said to the kids. "And, Dan, let me guess, you haven't practiced piano either."

"Not yet, Mom. You should see what the obstacle course looks like. It's really cool." Dan must have seen the look on my face. He and Mari hurried to set the table for dinner.

That left the real culprit, Brian. "A squirrel obstacle course? What were you thinking?" I snapped. "Don't we have enough obstacles of our own to deal with right now?"

"Who knows, it might even deter the little thieves, and it seemed like good fun," Brian said. "The kids will have a ball watching them. Lord knows, we could use some fun around here. I mean, a merry heart is good medicine, right?"

"We can all have merry hearts when there's less work to be done," I said, yanking the pan out of the oven. "Let's just eat and forget about the squirrels."

Easier said than done. Next morning, in the clear light of day, I got a good look at Brian, Dan and Mari's contraption. It was something all right. They'd set up three volleyball poles and run clothesline between them, the bird-feeder pole and a big oak tree. Here and there bungee cords hung with dried corncobs hooked onto them. It looked like some weird art project gone terribly wrong. Well, Brian put the ridiculous device up; he could take it down. I had more pressing things to do the next few days. Like vacuuming, cleaning the guest bathroom, wrapping gifts, cooking.

Brian, Dan and Mari chipped in, I have to admit, and by Christmas Day the house was in pretty good shape. Our guests started arriving. "My goodness," my sister-in-law said as we passed the big picture window that looked out onto the backyard. "What is that?"

"It's a...squirrel obstacle course," I said, through gritted teeth, ushering her quickly into the dining room, where I'd set up the table.

Soon the whole family was sitting around the dining-room table digging into their dinner. Mari and her cousin Lauren sat by the picture window in the living room, plates balanced on their laps, staring out back. They erupted into giggles.

"What's so funny, girls?" my sister called to them.

"The squirrels," Mari said. "You've got to come and see what they're doing!"

I got up and went to the picture window. A squirrel dangled from one of the corncobs on a bungee cord, desperately hanging on with his front paws while gnawing a kernel loose. Tail twitching, another squirrel perched on the trunk of the oak tree, contemplating the clothesline leading out to the bird feeder. He tested the line with his paws, chattered and chucked, then flung himself onto the line and inched his way toward the feeder. Upside-down.

Even I couldn't suppress a laugh. I felt someone's arm around me. Brian. It felt good, very good, to laugh. Brian's arm was warm and reassuring. I leaned against him, looked up at him and smiled. Sometimes the best medicine for an overwhelmed wife and mom is a husband with the good sense to see that a merry heart belongs at the top of the to-do list. Even if it takes something as crazy—and inspired—as a squirrel obstacle course to make her realize it.

# Checkered Past

*Marianna K. Tull*

$\mathcal{I}$ grew up in a simpler time and in a simpler place than our world is now, on a seventy-five-acre farm with many animals. It's the cats I remember most.

When I was five, Calico peeked out of my dad's overcoat pocket one evening upon his return from work, and I stared back with wide, eager eyes. She taught me how to love and be loved in return.

When I was a young girl, I opened the door for a scrawny little stray who was begging to be part of our lives. Tigger called forth from me pity and compassion. Later, when he became big and strong and the mighty hunter of our farm, spurning the front door to enter and exit boldly through the windows, he showed me how exciting it was to grow and change.

Tigger's proudest moment came the day he caught his first field mouse, hopped up on his accustomed windowsill and tried to utter his loudest "Please let me in!" What a decision! A very loud meow would let the mouse escape and dash his hopes of displaying his hunting prowess. With quiet humility, he would have his mouse but no one would ever see it. Growing into a mighty hunter wasn't going to be easy! Luckily for Tigger, my mother passed the window, praised him for his skill, but let him know the mouse was not welcome in the house.

Tigger could be a gentle friend too. My mighty hunter let me tie a baby bonnet under his chin and wheel him around in his doll buggy.

When I left the farm and became a mother, I thought I had left my cats and the lessons of my childhood behind forever. I had a life to build and sons to raise and so many new challenges on my mind. But as my sons grew, they let me know that parakeets, rabbits, gerbils and even a dog weren't enough. A cat had to be part of the family.

Blackie was a bold windowsill jumper. He never failed to appear on our neighbor's kitchen sill whenever the aroma of cooking liver assailed his pink nose.

Marmalade could be a fireball of energy when my youngest son wanted him to be. But he was happiest draped around my boy's neck as a huge, yellow fur piece, both of them quietly content.

Now that I am almost seventy-five, I find myself remembering the farm in greater clarity, like an old painting I have returned to, seeing fresh strokes of color. It is Checkers who stands out in sharpest relief.

He was huge and sleek with a startling black-and-white fur coat. He shared my grandmother's home, and they were indeed two of a kind. Both were very independent but easy to love and admire. I think Checkers enjoyed as many privileges as he, her grandchildren, did. His upholstered chair in the living room was a sight to see. One side was almost totally destroyed—his claw sharpener! He shared her bed, but never until the room was dark. Then he would stretch himself out full length, back-to-back with his loving mistress. The house they shared was a restored nineteenth-century stone farmhouse with a rather unusual water system. The water was pumped by a hydraulic ram from a spring in the meadow to an enormous wooden storage tank in the attic. From there it ran by gravity to the kitchen and bathroom of my grandmother's house.

One night, my grandmother was awakened by Checkers' loud meowing beside her bed. After several admonishments, she did not succeed in silencing him, so my grandmother followed him groggily into the hallway. Checkers ran immediately to the attic door, meowing loudly and pawing frantically at the door. Totally mystified and just a little annoyed, my grandmother opened the door and nipped the switch, flooding the attic steps with light. Just beginning to cascade down the steps was a very healthy stream of water, overflowing from the storage tank! A hasty call to my father, and the pump was shut off, preventing a disastrous flood. With crisis solved, Checkers sauntered back to the bedroom with his usual airy confidence, his detached mood indicating "It's all in a night's work." Ever after, I felt I should curtsy in deference to his uncanny knowledge of disaster looming on the horizon. Who knew what Checkers' next move would be?

When I sit at my typewriter, I try not to let Sparky, my amour of the moment, read this; and I silently mouth my apologies to all the other very intelligent and loving furry critters who have brightened my days. Sparky thinks she is the only feline who has ever shared my love and my life. She knows nothing of a ten-year-old girl who lived on a farm with many animals, and a cat named Checkers, who taught her that life was a difficult challenge and a foreboding journey; but there was tenderness and courage and mystery and quiet bliss with our feline friends to share the way.

# The Return of Roscoe

### Shari Smyth

*L*ight from an almost-full moon shone through the window on Roscoe, my old black Lab. He lay dozing by the fire, his graying muzzle twitching, his arthritic legs pawing the air in the long-forgotten rhythm of running. In his sleep he yipped, puppy-like.

"Hey, Roscoe, old boy," I said. Where were his dreams taking him? Was he tearing off again across a field and into the woods, hot on the scent of a squirrel? Or was he remembering that first year when I had such big plans for him? The wind howled down the chimney, scattering sparks from the fire. Roscoe woke with a jolt. Stiffly, he got up and hobbled over, resting his head on my lap. He'd never been a cuddler, but he liked having his ears scratched. In human years Roscoe was ninety-one. I was fifty-seven. We had come a long way together. I ran a hand along his bumpy bones. A contented sigh seeped from him. Really, is there anything sweeter than an old dog?

I lifted a velvety ear and touched the tattoo that marked him with the noble purpose for which he'd been bred. That was thirteen years ago, but it seemed only yesterday that I carried him, a wiggling eight-week-old bundle, into my house. With my four teenagers scattering to do their own thing, my work as a mom was winding down. Raising this little guy would keep me busy. At least he needed me to look after him. Inside the door, I pulled out a chair, sat the pup on my knee and gave him a little speech. "Somewhere out there is a blind person whose life you will change," I said. "My job is to love you, build your confidence, and teach you manners so you'll be ready for your trainer." Roscoe licked my face.

He had been born at the Guiding Eyes for the Blind breeding farm in Patterson, New York, not far from where we lived. I would have him for a year. Then he'd go back and be tested for the rigorous schooling it took to be a blind person's eyes. Roscoe's bloodlines were awesome, the folks at Guiding Eyes told me. They'd pointed out his parents' portraits, prominently, even reverently, displayed in their office.

"You've got a lot to live up to, Roscoe," I said, then couldn't help laughing as he bounded out of my lap and went after his rubber bone. "I'm going to raise you right so that all your good qualities come out."

Too quickly he grew from a sweet lap-sitter to a big-boned, handsome dog with a face full of expression. He had boundless energy. Even the kids couldn't keep up. Roscoe never got tired of playing fetch, his outsized paws pounding the turf. He was a graceful swimmer, steering with his tail after a ball in the lake. His bark was a deep woof, woof, woof.

"He's some macho dog," the FedEx man said, backing away as Roscoe, looking like a canine Arnold Schwarzenegger, accompanied me to the door. But his tail went thump, thump, thump.

Because he was a future guide dog, Roscoe went everywhere with me. The library, the supermarket, restaurants, church. He wore a blue Guiding Eyes jacket that fit well around his muscular black frame. Wherever we went people oohed and ahhed. The local paper even did a spread on him. "We'll be at this big guy's graduation," the editor promised.

What a proud day that would be! I pictured Roscoe leading his new owner across the stage to get their joint diploma. Sure, I'd miss him terribly. But knowing I'd helped him live up to his famous parents' bloodline would be well worth it.

In the meantime, I collected memories. The sly way Roscoe dropped his empty dish at our feet. Or averted his guilty eyes when he'd done something bad. The way he pranced with joy at the sight of his leash. And how he gave forth a long dramatic sigh when he settled down each night, as if the weight of the world was on his shoulders.

One summer Sunday, Roscoe was lying in the aisle at church, paws crossed, when Father Mark's sermon went into overtime. The congregation shifted in the pews restlessly. Sensing the general discontent, Roscoe tilted his face heavenward and howled. "Okay, I'm almost finished, Roscoe," Father Mark said to appreciative laughter.

Later, at the communion rail, Roscoe put his head down, repentant. Father Mark reached across and laid an affectionate hand on him. "Bless this dog, Lord, and prepare him for the future you have called him to."

The day before we were to return Roscoe to Guiding Eyes, I took him for a long walk around the lake. A sudden wind came up, churning the water with whitecaps, and there was a distant crack as though a branch had fallen. Roscoe lifted his head, his nostrils quivering. In the blink of an eye he was off, ripping the leash from my hand.

What on earth got into him?

I found him miles away on the other side of the lake. Wet and muddy. Long retriever nose plowing the ground. "Roscoe, you're never going to be a guide dog if you behave like this," I said. He looked up at me, the mischievous gleam in his amber eyes not all that different from my son Jon's when he skipped out on homework to go skateboarding with his friends. "All right, big guy, let's go home."

The next day I packed his things in a paper bag. Rubber bone. Teethmarked dish. Stuffed toy. Blue jacket. We drove to Guiding Eyes, Roscoe sprawled comfortably across the backseat.

The woman at the desk greeted us. "Oh yes, we know Roscoe," she said. "He's going to make a wonderful guide dog." Roscoe wagged his tail and looked up at me. He kept on wagging as they led him away. I gathered his old leash and took it to the empty car. I cried all the way home.

Two weeks later I got a phone call from Guiding Eyes. "Shari, we're going to have to release Roscoe. He's just not cut out for the program."

"What do you mean?" It was just as shocking as if one of my children had been expelled.

"He's a wonderful dog, but he's just too impulsive at times. Skittish too." Apparently during a training exercise, he'd panicked at a car back-firing.

"Was it me? What did I do wrong?" I'd been clear and direct in my commands. I'd disciplined him carefully. I'd been there for him.

"You didn't do anything wrong, Shari. Dogs aren't machines. They have their own personalities."

So my Guiding Eyes dropout came home. It was as if he'd never left. He went right to his spot in the back of the car when I drove carpool. At the kids' games I'd cheer and Roscoe would join in with his baritone woof, woof, woof, though I suspected he'd rather be chasing down the softball himself. He was part of our family, no question. Still, I wondered if I had failed him. Wasn't he meant for something more meaningful than warming the foot of our bed?

The kids graduated and left home. Instead of settling into a com-fortable, carefree retirement (from being a full-time mom, at least), I went through all kinds of ups and downs. One daughter's struggle with, and eventual recovery from, drug and alcohol addiction. Another's in-sistence on living far from home. A son's leaving his job to indulge his wanderlust. An unexpected move from New York, where we'd spent almost two decades, to Tennessee. A wrenching yearlong separation from my husband that ended in the joyful renewal of our marriage vows.

Now, sitting by the fire, I looked at my old friend Roscoe, sticking by me as he had through all those uncertain times. Keeping me company on long strolls through the unfamiliar Tennessee woods. Punctuating my solitary days writing at the computer with the thump, thump, thump of his tail on the rug at my feet. Laying his head in my lap just when I felt most lonely and unloved.

"You weren't meant to be a guide dog," I said. "God meant you for something else." I scratched Roscoe's ears. "He meant you for me."

# Rio's Journey

## Anne Watkins

_I_ stared in dismay at the scruffy green bird gazing back at me from his handmade wire cage. A surprise gift, I didn't know whether to be delighted or horribly upset. He was not much larger than a cockatiel and was dressed in a green suit topped off with dusky blue head feathers. All I knew about him at this point was that he was a blue crowned conure and that he was very sick.

His face was crusted with the thick stuff that oozed from his nostrils. His left eye was swollen and bulged in an ominous way. One wing had been clipped to the bone and the feathers were jagged all the way down to his body! It looked as if someone had used pinking shears on him. He was skinny and breathless and sneezed a lot. Still, there was something about this ragged bundle of feathers that captured my heart.

He climbed to the top of his cage, hung upside down and screeched at me. I couldn't help but laugh, and the more I laughed, the more he clowned.

I didn't know what kind of diseases he might have had and I didn't want my cockatiels and zebra finches to get sick, too, so I immediately quarantined him. I called the local avian vet and made an appointment for my new bird, whom I named Rio.

The next day, Rio and I visited the vet's office where I discovered that my poor little guy was in worse shape than I thought. He had a severe sinus infection and an upper respiratory infection too. To my dismay, the doctor also suspected psittacosis, a nasty, contagious disease that can kill whole flocks of birds!

"I'm sorry," she told me. "I don't think he'll ever recover, and if he does survive, he's so wily, you'll never be able to handle him."

She preformed the necessary tests, prescribed the proper antibiotics and vitamins, and made another appointment for us. Armed with instructions on how to catch Rio in a towel so I could work with him, I took my little patient and all his medical paraphernalia home.

Because he was so sick, Rio had to stay in his small blanket-covered travel cage, with a lamp close by for extra warmth. He was so confused and scared! For comfort, I sat next to his cage every available minute and talked to him through the blanket. When our first medication time came later that day, I found a worn-out towel, told myself to get it right the first time, and plunged ahead.

I stuck my hand in the cage, cornered a frenzied Rio and pressed him gently against the bars, careful to keep my fingers out of reach of his slashing beak. Then I tried to pull him out of the cage. Surprise! For such a little fellow, he sure had strong feet. I had to use my other hand to pry his toes off the bars.

I had already filled the dropper with medicine. I wondered how I would pry his beak open if he refused to take it. No problem. He clamped onto the dropper like an alligator. To my relief, he swallowed the nasty brown stuff and ran his tongue around his beak, tasting. It must not have been too bad, because he settled down in my towel-covered hands and gazed calmly back at me.

Over the next few weeks, it became evident that he liked me—and I had already fallen in love with him. He squawked whenever I was out of his sight, and would relax as soon as my towel-covered hand touched his back. His feathers lost some of their raggedness and his nostrils began to clear up. When the test for psittacosis came back negative, we celebrated! Originally given only a thirty to forty percent chance of survival, he was so improved that the doctor was confident that my little patient would recover fully.

By now, Rio was snatching treats from my fingers and rubbing his head against my face. Sometimes he would lick my skin or tug my hair. But we always played by his rules. He could touch me, but I couldn't touch him. If I tried, he warned me with a growl and pin-pointed eyes.

He needed exercise so I began letting Rio out of his cage every day. After a couple of botched attempts, he realized he couldn't fly and contented himself with climbing all over his cage and playing with the toys I made for him. When I wanted him to go back in, all I had to do was show him the towel, and he clambered back inside.

This wild little creature developed a trust in me that touched my heart. This became evident one day when someone he didn't know got too close. In a panic, Rio jumped off his cage onto my arm and ran up to my neck where he huddled, shivering, pressed against me.

Then came the day I had been dreaming of. I was feeding Rio bits of apple and trying to touch his beak each time he took a bite. He ignored my finger and nibbled his treat. I cautiously touched his beak with the tip of my finger. When he didn't try to bite me, I ran my fingertip up to the fringe of ducky blue feathers that edged his nostrils and gently scratched. Rio dropped his apple, fluffed his feathers and sat very still. Tears of joy streamed down my cheeks as I was finally granted the privilege of touching my precious feathered friend.

Those were the first steps of the long journey from being frightened strangers to becoming trusted friends. Today Rio's feathers are vivid and iridescent; his bright orange and black eyes shine with intelligence and spunk. He demands full body contact—no more of that silly beak touching for him! He solicits tastes of my food by asking "Is it good?" repeatedly until I give in and hand him a sample. He has an interesting vocabulary and loves to sing and dance.

Rio and I have been together for fourteen years now and he is a very special part of my life. It took painstaking months of patience and understanding for us to reach this point but I wouldn't trade a minute of our journey for anything in the world!

# The Little Marine
## Joan Drage

Tory, my cat, was five years old when I found him at the Denver Dumb Friends League. Five years later, I had major surgery, which kept me homebound for several months. A trip from the bedroom to the living room took a half hour—on a good day.

Overnight Tory changed from a pet to a guardian with canine actions. He was by my side constantly—literally my shadow.

When I was in the living room, he was on the ottoman—eyes at half mast, never even closed.

When I was in the bedroom, he was at the foot of the bed, ever alert.

When I was in the shower, he was sitting beside the tub.

When I was in the kitchen, he was in the doorway.

The only time he truly slept was when my mother or friends he trusted were over to make meals and visit—or when I was asleep.

If I were in the living room or kitchen and he needed some solid sleep, he would curl around the legs of my walker, because he knew I couldn't go anywhere without using it—thus waking him.

If we were in the bedroom and someone came in the unlocked front door, he would bound off the bed and be in full attack mode—until he saw who the intruder was.

Overnight, he transformed himself from a happy-go-lucky critter into a guard cat who took his job very seriously.

We called him the little Marine.

Though still friendly, he would not leave my side to solicit attention from visitors—something he used to run to people for.

If they wanted to pet him, they had to come by me, and I had to give him permission to be petted.

He used to love to play; however, he knew that I simply couldn't, so he never solicited it.

That was almost two years ago. To this day, I marvel at the transformation this wonderful creature made to care for me in my months of need. When things seem difficult now, I think of how my little Marine summoned the strength to support me, and things seem easier. He is an inspiration to everyone who knows him.

Although I once thought this would be impossible, his devotion has deepened our bond immeasurably. I now love watching him curled up and sound asleep—not a care in the world—or bouncing over to company and throwing himself on their feet so they have to pet him.

I deny him almost nothing today. He gave up six months of his life to selflessly serve and protect me—the least I can do is play ball for half an hour in the evening, or join him on the balcony on balmy days and quietly watch this noble critter have a well-deserved rest.

# A Note from the Editors

$\mathcal{G}$uideposts, a nonprofit organization, touches millions of lives every day through products and services that inspire, encourage and uplift. Our magazines, books, prayer network and outreach programs help people connect their faith-filled values to their daily lives. To learn more, visit Guideposts.org or GuidepostsFoundation.org.